The Gentle Rebel

The Gentle Rebel

The Civil War Letters of
1st Lt. William Harvey Berryhill
Co. D, 43rd Regiment, Mississippi Volunteers

Edited
by
Mary Miles Jones
Leslie Jones Martin

The Sassafras Press
Yazoo City, Mississippi

© 1982 by Mary Miles Jones
All Rights Reserved

Printed in the United States of America
Second Printing — September, 1983

Library of Congress Catalog Card Number: 86-60952
ISBN 0-9609692-0-9

CONTENTS

List of Pictures and Maps
vi

Dedication — Miss Mary Billy Miles
vii

Preface
ix

Saltillo — August 20, 1862
3

Grenada — December 23, 24, 1862
7

Vicksburg
11

Columbus — November 6, 1863—March 7, 1864
15

Montevallo, Alabama — May 1, 1864
21

Georgia Campaign — May 16, 1864—July 19, 1864
25

Atlanta — July 25, 1864—August 25, 1864
59

North from Atlanta — September 4, 1864—November 13, 1864
85

Tennessee — November 28, 1864—December 8, 1864
113

Appendix I — Family
137

Appendix II — Co. D, 43rd Regiment
150

Appendix III — S. Newton Berryhill
151

Index
157

LIST OF PICTURES AND MAPS

Mary Billy Miles
vii

William Harvey Berryhill
xiv

Map — Co. D Movements, April 25-July 4, 1863
13

Map — Co. D Movements, April-May, 1864
83

Map — Co. D Movements, May-October, 1864
84

Map — Co. D — Franklin, Tennessee
121

Map — Co. D Movements, October-December, 1864
122

Mary Elizabeth McDowell Berryhill
Noel Lamar Miles
136

**DEDICATED WITH LOVE
TO
MISS MARY BILLY MILES**
(See Appendix I — Family)

PREFACE

For the past three years, in spurts and at odd hours, I have been reading, arranging, and typesetting these Civil War letters, and, in the process, getting to know, admire, and love—yes, love—my great-grandfather. It's been a rare privilege and I am grateful for it.

After spending many, many hours with a magnifying glass and various paper and photographic copies of the letters, I believe every possible word has been deciphered, and that *all* the existing war correspondence of William Harvey Berryhill is contained in this book. Even pieces of letters which could not be put in their proper places are included at the end of the dated letters.

One task remains — to introduce the letters to readers so they will respond as I did to the quiet dedication of Billy Berryhill.

* * * * *

William Harvey Berryhill was thirty-four years old when, to quote the muster roll of Co. D, 43rd Regiment, Mississippi Volunteers, "This Company was organized at Bellefontaine, Mississippi, on the 25th day of April, 1862."

He was married and the father of five children, three boys and two girls. Two more girls were born during the war years — one in March, 1863, just a few months before her father was among the 30,000 Rebels who surrendered at Vicksburg, and another in July, 1864, while he was engaged in the Battle of Atlanta. Lt. Berryhill was killed in the Battle of Nashville on December 15, 1864, without ever having seen this youngest child.

W. H. Berryhill obviously wrote many letters home during his years of service with the Confederate forces, but not all were preserved. After the surrender at Vicksburg he was sent to parole camp at Columbus, Mississippi, and evidently spent some of the time between July, 1863, and May, 1864, at home, and it is assumed that many of his letters written earlier were disposed of during that time.

There were three letters dated in late 1862, one letter in November, 1863, and about forty letters dated from May until December, 1864, in the possession of Miss Mary Billy Miles when she died in April, 1979. The letters had been left with her by her grandmother, Mary Elizabeth McDowell Berryhill, widow of W. H. Berryhill, when she died on February 9, 1921. The letters were mostly to "My Dear Wife" and to their children, but others written to her brother, Ira, and to the Berryhill brothers had also been in her possession. After reading the letters there's no doubt but that *all* the letters were intended for his wife.

Mary Billy Miles had carefully kept track of the letters, which were folded, stacked, and tied with string into a neat little package. During her lifetime she had shared the letters with us and with others in the family and had, in fact, given one letter (written on March 7, 1864) and a sword sent from Nashville as a part of W. H. Berryhill's possessions, to Simon Turner, a grandson of the little girl Billy Berryhill never got to see. This letter was the only one discovered other than the ones Mary Billy Miles had, and which she had felt were too personal for general perusal and too painful to read herself.

After her death, my daughter, Leslie, and I spent many sad yet fascinating hours going through all her personal papers to determine their disposition. After reading again the letters from W. H. Berryhill, we felt they were too interesting, too important, too poignant to let fade away.

We were impressed with — and proud of — the character of the man who wrote these letters. His obvious love and concern for his wife and children was conveyed more by his quiet desperation when he did not get letters from Mary than by any written expressions of affection. He did not burden her with the hardships he was undergoing except through mere statements of fact, many of them humorous, and Mary obviously did not dwell on the destitution surrounding his family back in Choctaw County.

Instead, he wrote of his faith in Christ and his respect for His church, his love for the men of Co. D and others of his friends, and revealed through his letters his genuine humanity, his apparent lack of animosity toward anyone (including Yankees and Negroes), and his belief in States' Rights.

From a time in June, 1864, when he was put in command of the Pioneer Corps of Adam's Brigade, Loring's Division, he was more an observer than a participant in the Georgia Campaign, sometimes too far away to be sure of exactly what was going on, but not close enough to get caught up in all the rumors that spread so quickly through the troops. Usually he reported rumor *as* rumor.

His last letters indicate that he willingly left this safe assignment to assume command of Co. D after all its officers were killed in the Battle of Franklin. And, according to his obituary and hand-me-down stories, he was acting Captain of Co. D when he was shot in the head as he was leading them in line of battle on December 15, 1864, at Nashville, Tennessee.

*****

Our intention — Leslie's and mine — when we began our project, was to type the letters and make enough copies for all family members who were interested. We found many, many interested and enthusiastic relatives immediately. We talked and corresponded with Mississippi kin we had known all our lives — Simon Turner, Jewel Roberts, Edwin Glover, Mary McLemore, Lula Turner, all descendants of W. H. Berryhill's youngest daughter, Mary Lula. We are the descendants of Elizabeth Josephine (Lizzie) who was the second youngest. We renewed an acquaintance with Julie Gimler of San Francisco, granddaughter of William Albert (Willie), received much help and encouragement from Edward Bridges of Centerville, Tennessee, grandson of Laura Newtonia, and missed meeting Jack Berryhill, grandson of John, by only a few days! He was traveling on I-55 close to Yazoo City on the same day I was writing to him in Tulare, California, to see if by chance he had any of the letters. Hopefully we'll get to meet all the newly-found relatives soon.

That means that descendants of five of seven children know about the publication of the letters. The other two children have no relatives. Ira (Buddy) had one child who died in infancy, and he and his wife died shortly thereafter. Martha Euphrasia Ann (Mattie) — Aunt Mat to me — late in her life married a widower with children, but had no children of her own.

We've received a great deal of help, too, from Corinne Nelson of Horatio, Arkansas, whose great-grandmother, Sallie Ann, was a sister of W. H. Berryhill; LeNora Grimes of Hobbs, New Mexico, and the late Dr. W. Clyde Snow of Ralls, Texas, who descended from another sister, Martha Marcilla; Mae Berryhill, widow of Walter Berryhill who was a grandson of W. H. Berryhill's brother George (George has one letter in the book and is mentioned frequently); and Wendell McDowell and Carol McDowell Seymour, grandson and great-granddaughter of Ira McDowell, Mary Elizabeth Berryhill's brother and evidently best friend of Billy Berryhill.

Billy Berryhill must be interested, to put it mildly, in all the correspondence and conversation about him among his relatives. We failed to find only the descendants of one brother, John Wesley, while we were researching, but since the first printing have found them in and around Smithdale, Mississippi.

* * * * *

After realizing the full content of the letters, and the story they weave about one man—one family—during the Civil War, we decided that they deserved the first-class treatment, a real book. So this is a venture which my daughter, Leslie, and I embarked on with enthusiasm, and with the encouragement and full support of my husband, Wilson, and our son, Burke, my parents, Noel and Thomas Miles (Noel being a grandson of W. H. Berryhill), Leslie's husband, Richard Martin, and my sister, Marthajo Rademacher, her husband, Pat, and all their family in Illinois. Their two daughters, Susan and Nancy, each were given a letter by Mary Billy several years ago which are included in the book.

Leslie's planned participation in this publication was hampered somewhat by distance (she lived in Houston, Texas, for two of these three years), by the birth of two little girls within the same three years, and by our unwillingness to trust or wait on the mails. Leslie's most practical contribution was my Mother's Day gift in 1979 — a how-to book on self-publishing. And while she has perhaps missed some of the hours of real labor, she has also had to miss the joy of discovery which made it all so rewarding.

At first the letters were just words and paragraphs and pages, and I was more caught up in misspellings and lack of punctuation than in content. Early on, we had decided to make all the necessary corrections so that the reading would be smooth, but as I read them again and again, a continuity emerged that convinced me to let them speak for themselves.

During the course of writing and typing, and then typesetting the letters, I became quite comfortable with *quiett, untill, fiew, caverly, verry,* and others, and became quite taken with *shure* and *knap*. *Stoped* stopped me every time I read it, though, so I added the missing "p." I also made the sentences and paragraphs he couldn't afford to — his paper was scarce, sometimes he only had "one pine knot to write by," and who knows what kind of pen and ink he used. It certainly wasn't a ballpoint.

I also decided to use the word "and" in place of his little ampersand. The typeset "&" bears absolutely no resemblance to the little symbol he made in writing when he needed to conserve as much space as possible.

Someday we plan to study the history of those times to see if his "Sutler's Store" is really "settler's store," and to find out about coperas and balsalm. First things first, though. We've been long enough on the letters as it is. A refresher on Civil War history can come later.

* * * * *

As I typeset the final copy, I tried to be consistent with Billy Berryhill's consistency. That is, if he spelled it wrong, I tried to spell it wrong, too. If he spelled it correctly most of the time, I tried to spell it correctly all the time. As a consequence, Billy Berryhill and I have a secret. Only he and I know whether it's his misspellings or my typographical errors you'll find in this book!

M.M.J.

WILLIAM HARVEY BERRYHILL
May 28, 1828 — December 15, 1864

This picture, the only known photograph of W. H. Berryhill, was given to his youngest daughter, Mary Lula Berryhill Roberts, who never saw her father. Many years ago, a grandson, afraid that the heavy frame would cause it to fall and destroy the picture, nailed it to the wall in the living room of the Roberts home in Eupora, Mississippi. Miss Jewel Roberts still lives in the Roberts home. (Shortly after the first printing of this book, the picture crashed to the floor — *without breaking the glass, the frame, or damaging the picture.* It is now hanging properly.)

The Gentle Rebel

The Civil War Letters of
1st Lt. William Harvey Berryhill
Co. D, 43rd Regiment, Mississippi Volunteers

altillo

April 25 to August 31, 1862
Camp Little, Co. D, 43d Regiment

This company was organized at Bellefontaine, Mississippi, on the 25th day of April, 1862, and marched from there on the 5th day of May to West Point, a distance of 45 miles. From there it was transported by rail road to Prairie Station and marched by land to Aberdeen, a distance of 8 miles, where it remained until the 25th day of May when it marched to Okolona, a distance of 20 miles, remaining there on post duty until the 7th of July. From there it was transported by rail road to Gainsville, Ala., stopping there until the 16th day of August, 1862, when it was transported to Saltillo where it is at the present time.[1]

---

1. The troop movement records are from Confederate Army records of Co. D, 43rd Regiment, on file in the Mississippi Department of Archives and History, Jackson, Mississippi, and are included to smooth the transition between letters and provide factual details omitted in the letters.

Saltillo, Miss., August 20th, 1862

Dear Brothers George, John and Newton,[1]

    I address this letter to you all from the fact that I have not an opportunity to write to you all separately. I have nothing either that is interesting. But believing that a letter from me will always be a welcome visitor even if it brought you no news but the fact that I was still alive. I have been in fine health for the last 2 weeks untill today. I have a bad bowell complaint which makes me feel very bad, but I am able to be up and attending to my business.

    We were out on general review this morning. I never saw as many men at one time before. There was four brigades on the field and I suppose that there was some 10,000 or 12,000 men present. It was a sight worth seeing. We were reviewed by Gen. Price [Pap], he is a splendid looking old fellow. I would suppose him to be about 55 years of age. His face does not appear to be more than 45 but his locks would indicate that he was at least 75. We are in a Missouria brigade for the present [the 3d Brigade] commanded by Gen. Green of Missouria. He is about the same age of Price or perhaps a little older. He looks more like Jo McBryde than anybody that I know of and about such a size man. Gen. Price reminds me of Parson Walton and about such a size man but not so tall as Elder Walton was, I don't think, but I did not see him on foot, therefore I could not judge so well of his height. There was other Brigadier Gens. present but I could not distinguish them from the Cols. and Majs. for our Lieutenants all out-dress the Gens. Gen. Price was very plainly dressed and Gen. Green is as plain as an old shoe. So you see I have seen a live Brigadier and a live Major Gen. that I know of. Our Col. was the splendidest looking officer on the field and he has such a voice that he attracted the attention of the whole division.

    I have seen and talked with a live Yankee. He was a prisoner and a young man of good sense. He did not appear to think that the North could ever whip us. He was trying to fix up to get released on parole. I think that he got taken prisoner on purpose to be parolled so as to get home. They say that they do not want to be exchanged for if they are they will have to go into the army forthwith.

I do not think that we will stay here long for everything seems to indicate a forward movement. We drew 30 rounds of cartridges yesterday and everything seems to be fixing up generally. Some of the army has already gone up as far as Guntown. The enemy are committing a great many depredations in the county around Corinth and in fact everywhere in Tishomingo and Tippah that they dare to go, such as stealing negroes and destroying crops and everything that they can find and starving the widows and orphans to death. I think that they intend to fall back and are going to lay the country in waste before they start and as they go so as to prevent pursuit from the Confederates. The troops here look very well and I am informed that the health of the army is wonderfully improved.

We are required here as we were at Gainsville to keep everything swept up as clean as a parlor. We are not allowed to throw down within the lines a piece of bread, bone or trash or any kind. We have to take up everything and take it clear out of the encampment. We are encamped right in between 2 Missouria regiments, about ½ miles from Saltillo. I think that this is a healthy location. It is a high dry country, but there is a miserable swamp not far off.

I got the letters sent me by the hands of B. H. Vance. John's letter requested me to write to him at Bellefontaine and if he was gone it could be forwarded to him. Now if John is gone send this letter to him where he is, but I want it sent to Mary first so that she can hear from me as often as possible. I shall write to her in a fiew days but the mails are so uncertain that I cannot tell when she will get it if she ever does. I hope that John will be discharged for he is not able for service.

If we leave here I will have to leave my trunk. I will try to leave it with someone and will let you know so if any of you are passing this way perhaps you can get it and send it to Mary. Tell Father and Mother that I would like to see them but I do not know when I shall have that pleasure. They must remember me in their prayers.

I want you all to write to me often for I very seldom ever get a letter from any of you. I have got but one letter from Mary that has been mailed yet. I suffer a great deal of uneasiness about Mary and the children. I fear that her foot will never get well. I wish that you would all see that she has proper medical treatment and advise with her often and do all you can for her and it will be long remembered by me.

Your Brother,

W. H. Berryhill

---

1. W. H. Berryhill's brothers living at this time—George Washington, John, and S. Newton Berryhill. Another brother, Thomas Jefferson (twin of George Washington) died in young adulthood. For additional information on S. Newton Berryhill see Appendix III.

September and October, 1862

Remained in Saltillo about three weeks and then marched to Guntown and remained there about fifteen days. Marched to Baldwin, Miss., to Iuka, from there to Corinth and from there to this place, Waterford, Miss., where it is now encamped.[1]

renada

November, 1862

This company since last mustered has marched from Waterford, Miss., to Abbeville, Miss., about 12 miles. Left there on the first day of December. Marched to Grenada, Miss., about 65 miles . . .[2]

---

1. Muster records show that W. H. Berryhill was "at home sick" in September and October, 1862, so he may have missed the Battles of Iuka and Corinth even though Co. D participated in them. He does not mention either encounter in any of the letters.

2. According to T. T. Smith, who was with Co. D from the fall of 1862 until late 1864, the 43rd Regiment intercepted Federal troops at Holly Springs and again at Coffeeville as the Yankees were attempting to destroy the Mississippi Central Railroad. The Federals returned to Memphis and the 43rd, including Co. D, went on to Grenada.

Camp Rogers, Tuesday, Dec. 23d, 1862
My Dear Wife,

 I am all right now. The papers that Ira[1] brought set me all right twenty minutes after Ira got here.

 Mary, as regards boarding Maj. Corbett and Lady, I hardly know how to advise you. Probably it would be best for you to take them in if they are willing to pay you enough to justify you in doing so. We boarded them last year at eleven dollars per month but then we could get meat at 8 cts. Now it is double that price. We could get salt at our door for one dollar per bushel, now it is twenty times that price. Sugar is at least five times as high. Rice is at least three times as high and everything else in proportion. Molasses is three or four times as high and c. Thus you see that the price of eatables are from two to twenty times as high as they were when we boarded them before, and you know that when we summed the whole of our boarding matter up that we came out losers, or at least we did not make anything by it and we are not able to do such things for accommodation. Now while you have to pay from two to twenty times as high for provisions, I do not suppose that the Maj. would be willing to pay double on his board. And then you would have to give up your parlor again, which would crowd you very much shure. But then on the other hand you would have good agreeable company for from past experience I do not think that you could find two persons in the state with whom you could get along so well. And then I should not be so uneasy about you for I would know that you were not by yourself and they were always so kind to our children and our children love them so well.

 Now, Mary, I have summed the matter all up, but still I am unable to advise you what to do. At all event I do not believe that you could save yourself to have them at less than $20 per month and furnish a room for them and not less than $18.75 no how you can fix it. You know our past experience in boarding. You know that we lost our labor and promised ourselves that we would not do the like again, but whatever you do in the matter will be all right with me. So act for yourself.

December 24th

Mary, I have been very unwell for several days until last night. I rested very well and feel well this morning. I want you to send to Newton and get me 2 or 3 bottles of Balsalm and send it down by anyone passing so that I may be prepared for <u>any other severe attack of bowell complaint</u>.

I send you $100.00 by Ira which you can use as you think best. You had better procure plenty of pork. If you board the Maj. and lady you will need 1600 lbs. If Nolen has rice you had better buy a good lot of it and get everything that Corbet has to sell that will do to eat, such as chickens, turkeys, pigs, and c. and c., but you will not need peafowls.

Mary, I do not know what more to write now. Ira can tell you all about how we are fixed up in camps. I will have to go on dress parade in a fiew minutes. The cannons are firing in a hurry now on the river about town. I do not know what it is for but I suppose it is in honor to President Davis for they have been looking for him for several days and I expect that he arrived last night. I must go. Goodbye, Dear Wife.

W. H. Berryhill

Mary, I am off of parade now and I will write you a fiew more lines for Ira is not ready to start yet. If I could get to go to town I could get something for the children, but no man can get a pass to leave camps now. However, Ira will go by town and try to get a dress for Laura[2] and some candy for the children and yourself, too.

I have no idea when I will get to come home. I am sending you nearly all the money that I have but I expect to draw again in a fiew days and then I shall have enough to do me and perhaps can send you a little more, but I will not draw more than fifty dollars the next time I draw, but I will try to furnish you with money as you need it, for officers can draw between pay days if they need it.

Mary, write to me often. Tell me everything that you can think of for you can tell more on one sheet of paper than I can on two. Has your potatoes all rotted yet. How do you do for meal. Do you get any eggs and butter and c. and c.

Mary, kiss all the children for me and kiss Mattie[3] a half dozen times. Continue to pray to God for us all. Keep up your spirits. Tell the children to be good to you for Pa's sake. So goodby again, Dear Wife.

W. H. Berryhill

Tell Mrs. Snow that Bud is well.[4]

---

1. Ira McDowell, Mary's brother and evidently W. H. Berryhill's closest friend. W. H. and Mary E. Berryhill named their first son, Ira Jasper (Buddy) for him.
2. Laura Newtonia, first child of W. H. and Mary E. Berryhill. (See Appendix I for further family information.)
3. Martha Euphrasia Ann Berryill, second daughter and fifth child of W. H. and Mary E. Berryhill, who expressed often her joy that her father had only three sisters to name her after!
4. There are several references to "Mrs. Snow and Bud" throughout the letters. In fact, in the last letter written on December 8, 1864, just one week before his death, W. H. Berryhill requested, "Tell Mrs. Snow that Bud is safe and well." We do not know exactly which Mrs. Snow and Bud this is.

**November and December, 1862
Chickasaw Bayou near Vicksburg**

This company was transported from Grenada on the 28th of December to Vicksburg, Miss., about 140 miles.[1]

**January and February, 1863
Snyder's Bluff, Miss.**[2]

icksburg

**May and June, 1863
Vicksburg, Miss.**

This company has since last muster marched from Snyder's Bluff, Miss., to Chickasaw Bayou, a distance of 6 miles. Came on May 3, left on May 17 for Vicksburg, a distance of 6 miles. Was in the seige of Vicksburg, commencing the 18th of May, 1863, and continuous. The company is here at present.

1. When Grant and Sherman began their movements to take Vicksburg, the 43rd Regiment was transported by train and then marched in the rain (see letter dated June 5, 1864) to Chickasaw Bayou, about six miles up the Yazoo River above Vicksburg. Federal troops had landed there to try to take Vicksburg and, according to T. T. Smith, "came out the next day, which was about the 1st of January, 1863. We had thrown up temporary works and gave them a warm reception . . . and drove them back under cover of their gun boats."

2. Early in January, Co. D with the 43rd moved on up the Yazoo River to Snyder's Bluff, guarding the river against passage by Federal troops. While at Snyder's Bluff, as reported by T. T. Smith, they were attacked by the Federal fleet of gunboats — thirteen in number — and succeeded in repulsing them, disabling three of the gunboats. They remained at Snyder's Bluff until May, and assisted in moving corn from the farms in the river bottoms between the Yazoo and the Mississippi Rivers.

VICKSBURG, MISSISSIPPI, JULY ....7.... 1863.

To All whom it may Concern, Know Ye That:

I, *W. M. Berryhill*, a *1st Lieut.* of Co. *K* Reg't *43rd Miss.* Vols., C. S. A., being a prisoner of War, in the hands of the United States Forces, in virtue of the capitulation of the City of Vicksburg and its Garrison, by Lieut. Gen. John C. Pemberton, C. S. A., Commanding, on the 4th day of July, 1863, do in pursuance of the terms of said capitulation, give this my solemn parole under oath—

That I will not take up arms again against the United States, nor serve in any military police or constabulary force in any Fort, garrison or field work, held by the Confederate States of America, against the United States of America, nor as guard of prisons, depots or stores, nor discharge any duties usually performed by Officers or soldiers, against the United States of America, until duly exchanged by the proper authorities.

W. M. Berryhill

Sworn to and subscribed before me at Vicksburg, Miss., this .... day of July, 1863.

.... Reg't .... Vols,

AND PAROLING OFFICER.

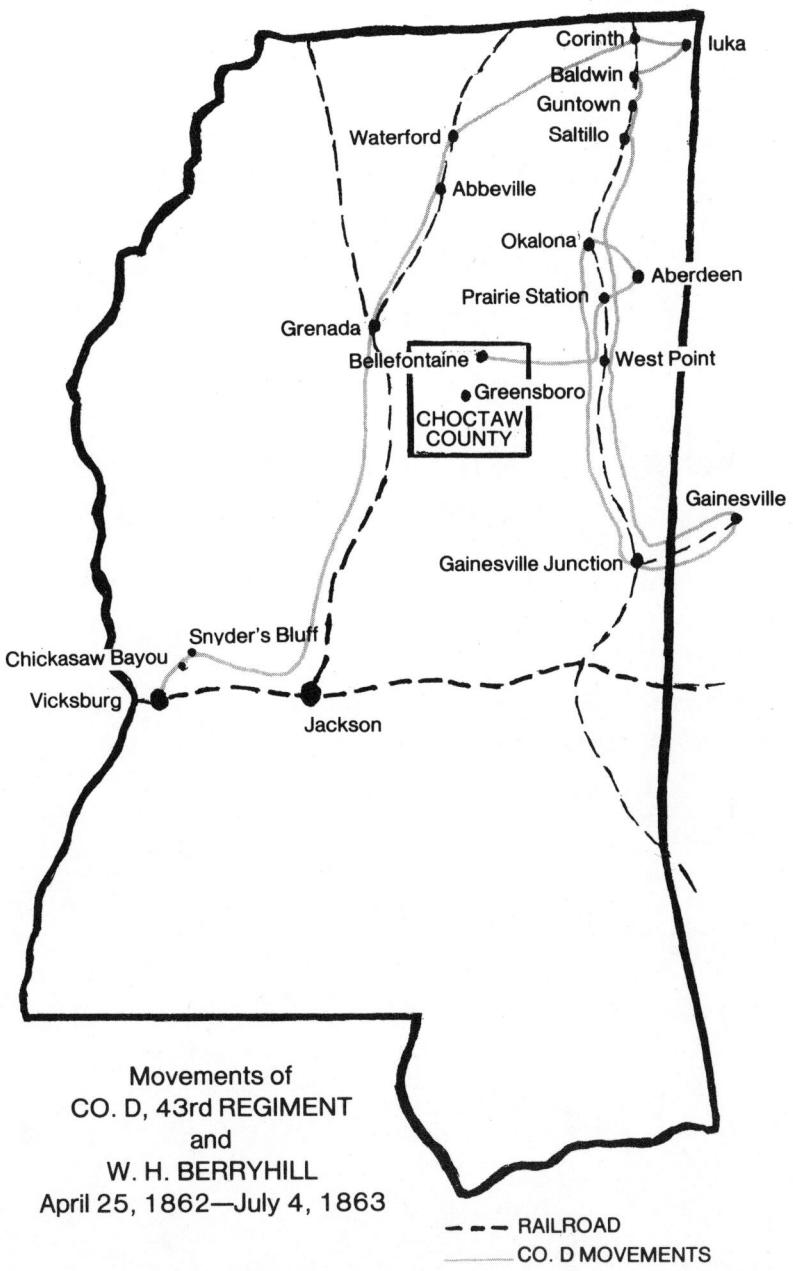

Movements of
CO. D, 43rd REGIMENT
and
W. H. BERRYHILL
April 25, 1862—July 4, 1863

– – – RAILROAD
——— CO. D MOVEMENTS

Columbus

June 30 to October 31, 1863
Columbus, Miss.

This company was all captured in the City of Vicksburg, Miss., on the 4th day of July, 1863, except those indicated not paroled; paroled and marched through the Federal lines on 11th and 12th July to Raymond to Brandon and thence to Enterprise to parole camp and were all furloughed for 30 days and ordered to report to parole camp, Columbus, Miss.

November and December, 1863
Parole Camp
Co. D., 43rd Regiment

Columbus, Mississippi

Columbus, Miss., Friday, Nov. 6th, 1863

My Dear Wife,

As Lieut. Spencer is going home I will write you a short letter to let you know how I am. My health is as good as usual. Yesterday was a very disagreeable day. It rained all day but the weather is fair this morning and a little cold. Mary, I have drawn one month's pay $90.00. I send you fifty dollars by Lieut. Spencer. You can use it as you see proper. I expect that you ought to have corn and fodder for your cows. Arch Holmes says that he will let you have a load of corn at one dollar per bushel when he gets home but I do not know when he will come.

Mary, write me when you get this letter and let me know whether you have been able to get any shoes for yourself and children yet or not. If you have not I will try to get them here, let the cost be what it will. I came very near getting you a pair of shoes a fiew days ago at 45 dollars. That would be a tremendous price but I prize your health more than I do Confederate money.

Mary, I think that you might have written to me by this time for this makes 12 days since I left home. Mary, do write often for this Parole Camp is the most dispicable place that I ever saw and it will do me good to read a letter from you. Mary, it is a most outrageous thing to compel men to stay in parole camps doing no good for the Government, for themselves, nor for nobody else but on the contrary an injury to all. There is but little control taken of the men and they drink and whoop and yell so of a night that there is no chance for a man to sleep. If it is not stopped very soon I shall complain to Gen. Ruggles and if he can not stop it I shall hunt me a boarding house and Co. D may go home for what I care. The men were tolerable still last night, having worn themselves down the day and night before. I think that we will have some regulations here in a day or two as Col. Banks says that it must be stopped. If a fiew of the leaders were put in the guard house the thing would be stopped at once. I am proud to say that not one of my company has participated in any of the sprees and everyone of them are down on it. I think more of Co. D than I ever have before and would not swap it for any company in the regiment.

The legislature is moving along slowly. I thought at first that they would hurry things through as their expenses is more than their pay, but my opinion is that they intend to increase their pay in proportion to their expense. We will see if I am right in the end. I attend their meetings every day. Sometimes it is interesting and sometimes very dull.

I send you some papers--one containing the Governor's message. I send you 2 oz. of Indigo for which I paid $3.00 per oz. making $6.00. Copperas is worth $1.50 per lb. and c.

Mary, I am so interrupted this morning that I can neither spell nor compose, so I will close for this time. Mary, pray for me for I am getting very cold in religion. Pray that I may be warmed up. May God bless and protect you.

W. H. Berryhill

P. S. Kiss the babies for me.

Columbus, Miss., Monday, March 7th, 1864

My Dear Wife,

    I expect some of my Co. will go home this morning and I write this letter to send by who ever goes. We are dismounted and our horses are turned over to Forrest except the private horses and they have nearly all been run off by those who owned them. I do not look for many of them back soon. All that had horses in my Co. left on yesterday except W. H. Farmer and T. T. Smith. I expect that one or both of them will be sent home with their horses today.

    I never have seen so much dissatisfaction in the 43d before. A great many have deserted and gone off to join the caverly some where. I sent you one of my watches. I gave the pistols that I brought from home for it. It was a lucky thing that I got the pistols off my hands when I did for if I had them now they would be a perfect dead letter on hand. I paid $45 for the pistols. I paid $5 to the watch maker to get the watch regulated so the watch has just cost me $50. I could sell it for three times that amount, but I do not want any more of the taxable Confederate money. I prefer to wait for the new issue. You can keep the watch running if you wish to do so. Wind it up every morning or every night. If I should never return you may give it to Buddy.[1] I sent the locket and my trunk key by Tom.[2] I hope you have got it.

    The boys who owned horses went without leave from me or anyone else, but I cannot blame them for their horses were in danger of being impressed. Caldwell took my saddle, blankets, circingle, Martingales, bridle and halter. I did not see him start but he told some of the boys that he would leave them with Ira at Greensboro.[3] I want you to see to it immediately for Blant is so slippery that he may go up. The bridle and halter is made together and the martingales, bridle and halter are worth 20 or 25 dollars. I made it myself. The circingle cost $6, the blankets are two half blankets and the cloth you made me. George[4] sends his watch by Farmer to

Jon's care. You can send it to his wife. I sent my curry comb by Farmer. I   has gone to Bankston.

I am not very well but am up and about. I have had the worst cold that you most ever saw me have but I am getting over it now. I was   when   but I took which   me up for a day or two. I cannot write more now as Farmer is getting impatient to start. Be sure to write more often. I do not need anything that I know of now. We will leave here in a fiew days, I think. We have been ordered to Loring's Division and Featherston's Brigade. I do not like Featherston much but will have to put up with him. He is at Lauderdale Springs,   . You need not write to me any more at this place. Kiss the children for me,

Your affectionate husband,
W. H. Berryhill

Send Martha Ann's letter as soon as possible as George wants her to have it as soon as possible and before Gilbert comes.

1. Ira Jasper Berryhill (Bud and Buddy), second child and oldest son of W. H. and Mary Berryhill. See Appendix I for more information.
2. Tom was evidently one of two slaves owned by George Washington Berryhill, brother of W. H. Berryhill. Zack was the other. They apparently moved freely back and forth between Co. D and Choctaw County.
3. Greensboro was where W. H. and Mary Berryhill lived at the time he went into service with the Confederate forces.
4. W. H.'s brother to whom he wrote the first letter in this book, but who served with Co. D during the rest of the war.

Montevallo

December 31, 1863 to April 30, 1864
Montevallo, Ala.

This company since last muster left Columbus, Miss., on the 11th of April, 1864, transported from there to Demopolis by the steamer Robert Watson, from there to Selma, Ala., in the cars; thence to this place on cars. Arrived here on the evening of the 13th of April, 1864. The rolls of this company have not been expurgated until this muster since entry into service.

Montevallo, Ala., Sunday, May 1st, 1864

My Dear Wife,

    I received a letter from you some 4 or 5 days ago dated the 18th April. I presume it is the first one that you have written to that time for you do not speak of having written any other. I would have answered it immediately but it was too late in the week for you to receive it by the following Monday's mail so I put it off until today which will give you a later date from me and will receive it equally as early as if I had written you 4 or 5 days ago. I would write at least twice every week to you but you have but one mail per week, so you see that it would do no good to write more than once. I have written twice or oftener every week since I left home, but I presume that you get them by packages so in the future I will write but once a week and write early enough in the week so that you may get a letter from me by every Monday's mail. But if I meet with a chance to send you a letter by hand I shall always do so, it matters not how many I have sent by mail.

    I was glad to hear of your all being well except poor little John.[1] I fear that he will never have any health. You state, too, that your Mother is still having those bad spells. I thought when I was there that she was about to get rid of them. You wrote me that George Oswalt's place was advertised for sale and that you supposed that Ira had written to me on the subject. I had got two letters from him before I received yours but neither of them sayed anything about it. You say that you would be glad if I would make some arrangements to get the place. I would like to have it, but I do not know how to begin in the matter. In the first place I do not know when it is to be sold 2d I do not know who is having it sold and in the 3d place I do not know wheather it is sold as Oswalt's property or Polland's or as some one else

May 1, 1864   THE GENTLE REBEL

for my recollection about the land is that there used to be several claims set up to it. But you can get in to possession of all the facts there and ought to make the purchase if you find that you are safe in doing so. I have but little money on hand now, not having drawn any since I left home. I only left home with 27 dollars. I have collected $25 from those that were due me here and have loaned $10 of that to Bro. George. My expenses since I left home has only been $17, leaving me $20 in hand. Of my expenses $8.50 has been for paper and invelopes [just one half of the whole amount]. The Government is due me to this date $270, which I will not draw untill I can get the new issue. You can have the use of the greater portion of that. For I shall not need much money now.

    We are getting a plenty of bacon and corn meal now, in fact more than we eat. We get flour, peas and rice occasionally. I could buy flour for about two days in the week, besides what I draw, but I had rather save my money for you and my children to buy something to eat with than to eat it up myself. But I do get tired of eating fryed bacon by the week. We had some lettuce for supper last night which is the first thing like a vegetable that I have tasted since I left Columbus. How is your garden getting along. I hope that you are getting plenty of vegetables now and eggs, too, and a long time ago I recollect of hearing of something that they called Butter and Milk. I wonder how it tastes. Does any of it grow in your garden?

    Tell Ira if an opportunity offers to make that ca. for me, but if it is not made I am doing very well where I am. I have some aspirations to be a caverly captain.

---

1. Third child of W. H. and Mary Berryhill, and the second of three sons. (See Appendix I for more information.)

Georgia Campaign

Resaca

Calhoun, Ga., Monday morning, May 16, 1864

My Dear Wife,

Through the providence of an all wise God I am permitted to begin to write you another letter, but I don't know when I will have an opportunity to write to you again or even that I will have a chance before leaving this place. If I had time I could write you a letter of 20 pages. I wrote you at Big Springs as we were on our march to Rome, and then again from Rome. In the first letter I said that we were on the point of starting for Resaca but the orders were   troops had got on the train so we had a lay over until the next day at 2 o'clock. We arrived at Resaca that night at about 12 o'clock. We camped and rested untill next day [Thursday] about 9 o'clock when we were ordered in the line of Battle.

As this thing had begun out west of the town for a fiew miles, we waited for the enemy to make an attack for a fiew hours and went back to camp for we found that he was not going to fight us yet. In the evening we found that Gen. Johnston was falling back to where we were and that the enemy had all left his front and was coming around through the mountains to attack us. By the next morning we found that they were approaching very rapidly with an army of some 75,000 to 100,000 men but Johnston had got his army down in position and we all felt shure that we would whip him. The skirmishing began on Friday about 2 o'clock and was heavy until night. Hood's Corps on the right, Hardee on the center and Polk on the left. We had men enough to form three separate lines of battle.

Our brigade was in the front lines, Featherston in our rear. There was heavy charges made on our right and center time and again for two days [Saturday and Sunday] and were repulsed every time with great loss to the enemy and some loss to us, but I am not able to say how much but not near so heavy, for the enemy made the attack and our men could shoot them as they came and as they went. There was no regular attack made on our part of the lines nor I do not believe they would have done so for we had a great position that gave us all the advantage of them and we were well entrenched. But there was a constant sharp shooting kept up all the while by both parties and a heavy cannonading. I made some narrow escapes. The enemy would not make a general fight at this place. Only just enough to make us believe that he was going to make the big fight there while he would cross the river below us and have us completely flanked and cut off from our supplies. But Old Johnston was too sharp for that for he vacated his position last night at [I] one o'clock and fell back six miles to or near to Calhoun where we are now, waiting for the Yankees to come up.

We burned the R. R. Bridge and other bridges across the river [Oostanaula] which will make their pursuit a little slow. I think that they are crossing somewhere below us but we are ready for them and I think that we will be shure to whip them whenever they will give us a general fight. But Johnston is not going to fight them only on ground of his own choosing if he has to keep falling back to the Atlantic Ocean. We have a splendid position here but I do not think that they will fight us here but will try to flank us again. We had one man killed and two wounded in the 43d. The man that was killed was joining to our Co. and in a fiew feet of some of our boys. Nobody hurt in Co. D. Some 8 or 10 killed and wounded in the 15th and as many in the 31st, but none of them from Choctaw but John Clark of the 15th who had his arm broken. The new recruits in our Co. looked

THE GENTLE REBEL   May 18, 1864

very wild when the shells began to burst and growl and howl around them. It made the Vicksburg boys laugh to see them look so wild.

Sunset Monday--I do not believe that the enemy will follow us. I am well.

Cassville, Ga., Wednesday, May 18th, 1864
My Dear Wife,

I wrote you two days ago from Jacksonville or near it and I   going   again   and fights   we were in line of fire when I wrote but the enemy made no direct attack upon us.

We moved from   at Jacksonville and marched 10 miles and had   10 o'clock tonight when we took it. We finally marched and arrived at this place 10 miles at sunrise this morning.

skirmishing from Resaca less than 30 miles. We marched as far in one day when we were going towards the enemy as we do in three days going from them. It is more a maneuver for position than a retreat. Gen. Johnston can and does repulse them when ever they advance upon us but says that he cannot get a decisive victory over them unless he can get them away from the mountain for if he defeats them near to the mountain they only have to fall back to the passes and gaps of them and we cannot pursue them any further. There has been fighting and skirmishing here for the last 2 weeks. Johnston is moving so slowly South that he appears to only be taking the enemy along. They ventured up to our rear at Jacksonville and were repulsed by Clebourn's Division. They came up with us again on yesterday evening at or near

Adairsville and were repulsed with considerable loss by Bates' Division. Bates ambushed his division on each side of the road and sent the caverly forward to skirmish with them and fall back untill they were drawn into the trap. The caverly pretended to be flying in confusion just at the right time which caused the Yanks to come in with a rush to come up with [as they supposed] the flying rebels, and the first thing they knew Bates opened upon them with his artiliary and infantry, which caused them to get back in double quick leaving a good many of the blue coated rascals dead in the road. I have heard nothing from the Yanks today but I suppose that they are moving on after us slowly. I do not believe that they will follow us much further. I expect that we will move still further south tonight.

    I learn that Johnston has his battle field selected if he can draw the enemy down to it and I do not think that this is the place, though it is a strong position as far as I can see. We have an immense army and have been reinforced by some 10,000 men since we left Resaca. My opinion is that we will whip them badly when ever it comes to a general issue. I hear it's going the rounds in the regiment now that the Yankees are not pursuing us today.

    Mary, I have stood the hardships of this trip better than I have ever done before. I have been in good health all the time. I have suffered considerable pain in my left foot in marching.

    Mary, I do not know that I have a rag of clothing besides what I have got on. I know that I have no socks but the ones that I have on and the toes and heels of them are out. I bought a roundabout coat which I have on. It is a coarse make. I bought me a domestic shirt for ten dollars but when we got to Rome my clothes were all dirty and I thought that I would have them all washed, but as soon as they were put into the wash tub we were ordered off, so I had to roll up the domestic shirt and I pr. drawers into a bundle, wet as they were, and put them in my saddle bags and throw them into a wagon and have not seen them since. I recon that they are rotten by this time [8 days]. My janes coat and old shirts are with them. I don't know when I will see the trains, and all may be lost by this time anyway.

New Hope Church

Near New Hope Church, 16 miles North of Dallis, Polk Co., Ga., Saturday, May 28th, 1864

My Dear Wife,

  I wrote to you last Sunday from Allatoona Mountains by W. L. Johnson. The next morning   hotest day you ever saw. We took up the line of march in a Southern direction but we marched to almost every point of the compass for several hours, but in the evening we were going nearly west. We marched about 4 miles, then camped for the night.

  Tuesday, the 24th, we set out at sunrise in a South East direction, but soon turned to the S.W. and by 12 o'clock we were going due West. We camped at one o'clock. This was in line of battle, too, for we were told that there was Yankees not many miles off. Later in the evening we heard cannonading some 10 to 15 miles off and in a due West direction. We marched some 12 miles this day.

  Wednesday, the 25th, we set out West and marched some three miles and halted in a field and stacked arms until 12 o'clock when we about faced, marched 1/2 mile, then turned due North, marched 2 miles, halted, stacked arms and set down to rest, made up fires to have an early supper before night. Some were gone after water, some were slicing meat to broil, I was parching old Regt. Coffee when heavy musketery opened some 2-1/2 miles North of us. We gathered up every thing and moved up the road a fiew hundred yards and stacked arms to await orders. We finished making our coffee and drank it when we heard the familiar word to a soldier, "fall in." We were into line in a minute for the small arms were rattling at a tolerable rate. We struck a double quick and trotted off a couple of miles in less time than I ever made before. I thought that we were going to run right into the fight but we were stopped some 600 yards from it and formed reserve lines of battle. It was now getting dark but the small arms were rattling like a tremendous hail storm and did not cease untill it was good dark.

It now set in to raining and we streached our sheets and blankets to keep us dry. It did not rain much and faired off by 10 o'clock and we were all fixing to sleep but that same word "fall in" sounded on our ears. We marched around to the front line near to the battle ground and we formed a line of fortifications hastily made of logs and fence rails piled up about as high as a man's waist which had been occupied by Hindman's division. Our men had repulsed the Yankees, capturing a fiew prisoners. Our loss was small. I do not know what the enemy loss was but as a matter of course it was more than ours for they made the charges and were repulsed, giving our men the advantage of killing them coming and going.

Thursday, the 26th, we commenced early in the morning to improve our works by cutting poles and piling them up as high and as thick as we wanted them. Nothing of interest took place this day, only skirmishing and sharp shooting, each army holding its original position so far as I know.

Friday 27th. Early this morning we began to throw up earth works in Co. D, the rest of the Regt. having completed theirs during the night. In a fiew hours we had splendid works. We have excellent fortifications all around so far as I have seen and I have seen some 4 or 5 miles of them. I do not know how long our lines are but I suppose they are some 10 or 11 miles long.

Nothing occured in the first half of the day worthy of note. Skirmishing, sharp shooting and cannonading all the while along the lines. In the after part of the day the firing became very heavy and the enemy made one of the most desperate charges of the war on Clebourn's Division. Our men lay concealed in the bushes until the drunken rascals came within a fiew steps of our works where they were killed by the hundreds. 496 were left dead in front of Gen. Grandberry's brigade and it is said that an equal no. was left in front of Loring's brigade. This is true for Col. Sykes has just come from off the field.

Lost Mountain

Near Lost Mountain, Cobb Co., Sunday, June 5th, 1864

My Dear Wife,

The last letter that I wrote was dated up to Thursday the 3d inst. Everything so far as I could see or know has went on about as I had described it to you for some days before my last. I think that I told you that the enemy were massing their forces on our right to try to turn that flank. The impression continued the same through Friday and Saturday. Last night we went to bed as usual, but had scarcely got to sleep when we were called up and ordered to pack up and be ready to march. About 10-1/2 o'clock we began what I had predicted in some of my letters--"a fall back."

The night was almost as dark as the coal pits and it had been raining for 3 days and was still raining. The mud was worked up to from 3 to 8 inches deep and was about as thin and soft as batter. You have no idea how fast 60,000 or 70,000 men and horses with wagons and c. will work up the mud when it is raining. Nor how fast they will pack it down when the sun is shining. But as I was saying we set out about 10-1/2 o'clock in the direction of Marietta or Lost Mountain, which is a lone mountain some 6 miles from where we started, and on top of which our signal corps occupied to watch the movements of the enemy. We had not gone more than a mile before our guides lost the road that we were to travel. So we had to about face and go back the way that we had come to get the right road if possible. We would move up a little, then stop and stand, sit or lay down in the rain a little while, then move up a fiew steps and then stop again untill I believe that soldiers, Generals and all, were lost in the darkness. We got into a road though that brought us off in a round about way, but I have no idea that it was the road that was intended for our division to travel, for I think that daylight found us less than 4 miles from where we started. We stopped where we now are about 8 o'clock and I have no idea that we are five miles from where we started and not more than two from some parts of our old works.

Day found us all wet and the muddiest set of fellows that you ever saw. When we stopped this morning a drink of whiskey was given to all that would drink and the majority drank, and from the way that many of the poor fools smacked their lips they appeared to think that one small drink had fully paid them for their night's toil in the rain and mud. Our Gens. do not suffer enough whiskey issued to hurt any man, but then on the other hand I do not believe that it does any one good. I and others who do not drink at all stand the fatigue just as well as those who do. But I will not complain at the whiskey rations for I have never known but 4 rations to be issued.

Last night was next to the worst night that I ever traveled. We had a worse time the night that we marched from Vicksburg to Chickasaw Bayou in Dec. 1862. We have had one shower since we stopped here, but we have all dryed ourselves, cooked and eaten dinner and taken a knap and are all right again. The most of the regt. are asleep now but I wanted to write you a letter so bad I made my knap very short.

I do not know wheather Johnston is going to make a stand here or not. We are getting far enough down now for the enemy to dread us as bad in their rear as we do them in ours. I am well and have got so that I can stand the camps as well as anybody. Nobody hurt in Co. D, but 2 killed in the Regt. since we came to Ga.

Mary, I have never heard wheather you have got my trunk from Columbus or not. If you have not write or get Ira to do so for you to Wesson to know if it has come to Bankston and to Murdock at Columbus to know if he has ever sent it to Bankston.

My Dear Mary, I would almost give my life to be at home with you for the next six weeks to   yet there with friends to you or myself and I know that you do not But be assured, my dear wife, that I will come just as soon as I can get permission to do so. If Johnston is victorious here we will be sent back to Miss. as soon as these fights are over. I do not know wheather the Yankees are pursuing us today or not. If they do we may give them a brush here tomorrow.

Mary, be of good cheer and pray for me constantly and all will be well. Tell the children that I think of them every one many times a day. I dreamed of seeing little Lizzie[1] and having her in my arms a fiew nights ago. Mary, I can only sigh and pray for home sweet home. I have got no letter from you or Ira since those by Shaw dated 4 weeks ago. George is well. We have sunshine this evening. I am your affectionate husband.

W. H. Berryhill

1. Elizabeth Josephine, sixth child of W. H. and Mary Berryhill, born March 29, 1863, while her father was at Snyder's Bluff near Vicksburg.

Pioneer Corps

Hd Qrs Adams' Brigade
Division In Field June 28, 1864

Special Order,
No —

Lieut. Berryhill of Co. D 43rd Miss. Regt. is hereby detailed to take charge of the Pioneer Corps of this Brigade and will report at once to these Head Qrs for duty.

By order of
Brig Gen Jno. Adams

E. H. Gregory
A.A.G.

To
Lieut. Berryhill
Thro.
Col. Harrison

Rennesaw Mountains

Three Miles South of Marietta, Tuesday, June 28th, 1864
My Dear Wife,

I wrote to you by Notley Gore last Tuesday, the 21st, which I hope that you have got, and then again [by a young Mr. Thomas who lives near Bankston] on the 24th, this one was to be mailed at Bankston. I hope that you have got it also. But least you have not got it I will tell you again as I did in that one that I have been assigned to the command of the pioneer corps of Adams' Brigade. I repeat this on account of the many fears and great anxiety that you feel for my safety.

I have just got your letters of the 12th and 19th inst. It was a sort of double letter but it did not tire me in the least to read it, and read it again. I regret to see that you are imagining so many horrid wounds and deaths as having come upon me and I imagine that the news of my assignment to this command of the pioneer corps will be gladly received by you, as the danger of being killed or wounded is not half so great as it is in the line service though sometimes we are in dangerous places but never go into a fight or use arms. But there is no glory or fame attached to it. My Business is to make roads, bridges, fortifications and c. I was assigned to the command on the 21st inst., just one year and 2 days from the time that I was taken from my Co. and assigned to the command of another. I hope that I will not meet with the misfortune to have to surrender this one fifteen days after taking charge of it as I had to do before.

I am properly entitled to a horse but do not know that I will get my rights as there are many things that men are entitled to in the army now that they do not get. But you may rest assured that I will see the general later but that I will have something to ride if it is nothing more than a billy goat.

    I was at the 43d regt. two nights ago and Col. Harrison told me that the General had expressed himself to him as being highly pleased with me. As a matter of course you know that this gives me the big head. I have a good deal of hard work to do or rather to have done [I need not tell you that I have taken to work] but I am not subject to the orders of everybody. I reckon after this I will have to give up the daily account of matters and things as they take place as I have been doing in my letters heretofore, for I shall frequently be away from the brigade for several days at a time, but I will give a short item of each day proceeding since my last up to this time as far as I have heard.

    It may be several days before I finish this letter as I am expecting again that Tom will start home in 4 or 5 days and want to send this by him. My last was up to Friday. Saturday, 25th. All was quiet on the right and but little firing on the left. Sunday, 26th. Considerable firing on the left before daylight, but after sunrise it was unusually still throughout the day, more so than we have had at any time before this when the enemy were in our immediate front.

    Chaplin Stone preached to the 43d under the shade of a tree without being disturbed, as only one mini-ball intruded itself into the congregation, which came in while the preacher was at prayer and darted into the ground in the midst of the crowd. At about 10 P.M. pretty heavy firing began with the pickets in front of Adams and growing more rapid on the left as the night advanced, continuing untill the dawn of day of Monday the 27th when it slackened to some extent.

    I neglected to state that I was ordered to the rear on Sunday after 12 o'clock to begin work on a new line which was being marked out some five miles in rear of the line at Kennesaw Mountain. I walked out here and then over the woods marking out the lines untill near sunset and then set out and walked back to camp with orders to report back here by daylight next morning. You may be shure that I was tired when I got in that night, but after I got in I received new orders which was to report to Gen. Featherston at sunrise the next morning [Monday, the 27th] which I did. I was directed to come out here and put up several bridges on a little creek between our main line and picket line and to throw up rifle pits on the line that we had marked the day before. Soon after I left a tremendous cannonading began and continued throughout this day. I have not heard it equaled since the days of the siege of Vicksburg. The Yankees made some of the most desperate charges of the war, in some places coming right up to our works and planting their flags on them. They were repulsed with tremendous slaughter. The heaviest of the fight was on the left center and left wing and on the extreme right, it being the right of Loring's division, Hood having gone to the left. Scott's brigade formed the right of Loring's division, Featherston the center, and Adams the left. They made a very heavy charge on Scott, driving in his pickets and occupying their pits and advanced on his main works in three lines of battle to within 200 yds. of our lines when Scott opened upon them with small arm and cannon with shell, grapes and canister, which I am told mowed them down by the Wholesale. I with my corps had assisted to plant a battery of 4 guns on Scott's right which I am told completely infiladed the enemies lines, completely ruining him. They charged Featherston's picket only driving them in on the right which was unnecessary on account of Scott's having gone in. They charged Adams' pickets but were repulsed.

Mary, I am five miles away from the scene of action and I hear a thousand things about the fight. So I cannot give you a correct account of it now. I may say more about it before I am done. We captured some prisoners, several stands of colours, and I am told that the dead are almost in piles between the mountains. George Oswalt killed Estus Bridges a fiew evenings ago while on picket. George was on outpost, Bridges was sent out in front to reconnoiter and when he came in front of George he mistook him to be a Yankey and shot him. It was getting dark . . .

Today [Tuesday] has been as still a day as Sunday was, at least so far as I can hear. There has scarcely been a cannon fired today. I am rather too far off to hear small arms unless they are fired very rapidly. I should have remarked in my account of yesterday's fighting that our men did a great deal the most firing of cannon owing to the fact, I suppose, of their men being so close to our lines. It is the impression now that the army will not fall back to this point. And, in fact, I do not know that it was positively the intention to fall back here unless it became absolutely necessary. Indeed, Gen. Loring told us when he started us out to begin the work that he only wanted to have it ready to fall back upon if necessary.

You ask me why it is that I do not mention Capt. Gilbert and say that something shurly must be wrong with us. I can assure you that there is no misunderstanding with us and that we are as intimate as we ever were in our lives. If you had gotten all my letters you would have found that I did mention him. But I expect that I have been too neglectful in mentioning the men of Co. D, but really I did not see the use of doing so for they all write constantly though not so often as I do. I suppose that I am a little selfish and when I begin to write I am so much absorbed in thinking of you that I write mostly of myself and of things concerning you and the children and our own affairs. Capt. Gilbert is well but looks smartly broken down. Lieut. Spencer is standing the trip as well as any of them and is as good pluck as any need, for he never appears to get scared or excited on no occasion, but is just Jimmy in a fight or out of it. A. McVey, D. Moore, Thos. Gilbert, A. Holmes, B. F. McCain, Blant Caldwell and J. A. Norris are at the hospital. Holmes wrote us that he was getting well and would be in soon. Blant has got well some time ago but is ward master in the hospital where he was so I do not look for him soon if ever. Anglin, Klutts, Capps and W. H. Farmer were in hospital but have returned.

You want me to hunt up David Keneda. If I knew his regiment I could find him but it is no use to ask me to look up a man unless I know his regt. David is here for a Chas. Harris of my Co. who lives near Levi Spencer told me today that he had seen David since we came to the Kennesaw Mountain. Mr. Harris says that 4 of Livid's negroes had ran off to the Yankees.

George is in tolerable good health and is still keeping the Col.'s horses. We have had a week of dry weather and have got soap and washed up so that we look like a new lot. It is getting too dark to write more now. I will write tomorrow evening.

Wednesday evening, the 29th. We have been digging rifle pits all day. If the army should fall back we will have good works for them, but I do not like this position as well as I do the Kennesaw Mountain position. It has been very quiett today and it is hard to tell what the Yankees will try next. My present location is about 18 miles from Atlanta. I have a house to stay in here and am doing well. We get vegetables occasionally in their neighborhood and if I had money I could get anything of that sort that I needed. Gen. Johnston is procuring vegetables and issuing to the whole army occasionally. Georgia is the greatest country for apple orchards that I ever saw anywhere and we get apples and stew them every day. The men back on the lines do not come up with fruit often. I will be out here at least a week.

I notice that Laura does not like for me to insinuate that she does not write to me and says that she has written several times. I have got but the one letter, it was dated May 27th. I am glad to see that Laura is making some money by envelope making. I could sell a good large lot of them for her if I had them here.

If I had my trunk here now I would be all fixed up. You say that you have written many times in regard to getting my trunk home. This last letter is the first one that I have ever received that sayed anything of it. I hope that your Pa got my mattrice and bed clothing when he went to Mr. Embry's after corn as he had to go and come right by the house. I am sorrow that your Ma's health is still so bad. My Mother was in bad health some two months ago. No one has mentioned her health since then, though you have spoken of her in nearly all your letters.

Mary, you ought not to conclude that because I am in the army that I am necessarily bound to be killed. You say that there is ten chances for me to be dead to where there is one for me to live. There has scarcely ever been a battle fought where there was more than one out of five killed. I think you ought to have said just the reverse for I considered it all the time that there was 10 chances for me to escape where there was one for me to be killed.

Direct your letters thus -- Lieut. W. H. Berryhill, Pioneer Corps, Adams' Brigade, Loring's Division, Army of Mississippi, and they will go where ever I do.

Thursday, June 30th

Dear Wife,

I do not have time enough to write a whole letter at one time so I write a little every day. This way of writing makes a very disconnected letter and I may write the same thing twice for I sometimes forget what I have written from one day to the next. I am still having ditches cut through the woods. It keeps me busy to superintend 20 men's work. Mary, if all the ditches that the Confederates have cut since we left

Resaca were put into one continuous ditch, I could travel from here to old Choctaw. Cobb County is cut all to pieces and the people are completely ruined and brought to beggery. The lines that we are now making runs in some places through beautiful corn fields, gardens and orchards and c. Good dwelling houses are pulled down where ever they are the least in the way. The people flee from their homes leaving their all behind and their homes are pillaged as soon as they come to them and, in many instances, they are robbed before the people leave. It is heart rending to see how the people are suffering here. I feel so thankful that our Choctaw homes are not visited by the armies.

The enemy made a desperate charge on the left wing of our army this morning at 2 o'clock. It was south of Kennesaw Mountains and on the road leading from Dallis to Marietta. I am five or six miles off but the roaring of the musketry awoke me as soon as it began. It lasted I suppose about an hour. A fiew minutes of the time I thought was the most rapid that I ever heard. I hear it said today that the enemy advanced in 7 or 8 columns and got within ten paces of our works but were repulsed with heavy loss. I have not heard enough about it yet to tell you any of the particulars and I do not suppose that there is any person that can tell much about it for it was too dark to see many steps from the works. Things have been pretty quiett today up to this hour [one o'clock]. I ate a good mess of collards and pot licker for dinner and I am too stupid to write anything intelligible now so I will stop for the present.

Later-- Mary, I learn this evening that the heavy firing this morning before day was pretty much all negros firing and was all done at long range. We had a fiew men killed. I do not know what was done for the Yankees. The Yanks capture some of our men occasionally. They captured the most of an Alabama regt. not long since. Lt. John B. Davis that used to live at Greensboro was captured and I see in the paper that he had arrived at Nashville, Tenn.

We have been getting the best of the Yanks here for some time past. There was a great many Yanks killed last Monday by their charges on our lines. Reubin Hitt got his leg shot off a fiew days back. The 43d was on picket last Wednesday and got two men killed --one was in Co. A and one in Co. B. Our army is at least 100,000 strong and I will   . I can not write more now but will write tomorrow.

Kennesaw Mountains. July 1st, 1864, Friday

My Dear Wife,

Today at 12 o'clock I was ordered back to the front with my corps and we are now engaged in building the strangest kind of forts on our main lines. We are making them 60 ft. square on the inside, the earth walls are 20 ft. thick with a deep ditch all around and the outside 12 ft. wide. I think that the work that we have been doing in the rear is all in vain for these works look like Gen. Johnston is going to make a death struggle here. It has been very quiett all day untill the last half hour with only about a half hour by sun the guns have begun to fire pretty rapidly. I believe that the Yankees are going to make a charge on our center which is where they made the effort last Monday.

I learn that Stewart has been made a Lieut. General and has taken command of Polk's Corps today. I think that Loring ought to have had it.

Mary, Tom is going home tomorrow morning and it is now nearly dark so I will have to close at the bottom of this sheet. I hope that you are doing well. Be shure to write me when Tom returns and as often as you can before he does come back. I am very uneasy about you now and shall be so until I hear from you again. I had a splendid place to stay out where we were at work and I hated to leave it. We had the best water that you ever saw — a spring similar to the Pace Springs and the old fields were full of blackberrys and dewberrys which you know I am as bad after as a child.

Mary, continue to pray for me for I think that your prayers are keeping me out of harm's way. It is getting dark here so that I cannot write this letter. Excuse mistakes. I want to see all the children very much, especially Lizzie. Tell Laura to send me a pack of her envelopes when Tom returns. It will be several days before I can write again. I am in good health. Yours as ever,
W. H. Berryhill

July 2, 1864

My Dear Wife, I think that the big fight is beginning this morning at daylight. It is now sunrise and very heavy skirmishing and cannonading is going on. I was ordered with my Corps 8 miles to the rear this morning at day break. I am now on my way. I am going to work on another picket line to have ready to fall back to if necessary. I am well. I had your letter sealed so I put this in a letter that George has written to Newton who will send it to you. Good bye.
Your Billy

The following letter was written by George Washington Berryhill to his brother, S. Newton Berryhill. and is the one mentioned in the above note from W. H. Berryhill.

One Mile North of Marietta, Ga., July 2d. 1864

My Dear Brother,

    I again resume my history of events commenceing the first of June. Wendsday, June 1st, nothing of importance occured during the day with the exception of sharpshooting on both sides. Kept poping away all day. Thursday, 2d, commenced raining to day. The Yankees have moved all their forces to the right and uncovered our left wing. But little skirmishing through the day.

    Friday, 3d, In front of Polk's corpse there was but little fighting. Gen. Hardee had a brush with the enemy late in the eavening and repulsed them with considerable loss. Saturday, 4th, Still raining. Roads almost impassable. A picket charge on Frenches Divission this eavening. Enemy driven back. At 10 o'clock at night rec. orders to fall back to Lost Mountain. Moved out of the ditches and then commenced a tedious nights march through rain and mud and dark! You could not see the next man before you. However by morning we had succeed in marching 4 or 5 miles from our old line.

    Sunday, 5th, formed a line of Battle and commenced fortifying. Our line now extends from the rail road east to Loss Mountain on the west. At one o'clock went up with Col. Sykes to the top of the mountains. The sight more than repayed me for the walk. The enemy's waggon train was plainly in view moving to our right and columns of smoke are ascending on their line of march supposed to be the burning of houses. Crops of all kinds are entirely distroyed.

    Monday, 6th Continued to throw up breast-works. Our scouts brought in several squads of Yankees. They also captured a Yankee mail containing a great many letters.

    Tuesday, 7th. Still at Loss Mountain and intrenching. Rain in an abundance. Saw cousin Jas. N. Campbell to day. He was in fine health. At 12 M took up the lines of march traveling the Marietta wall 4 or 5 miles. We turned to the left in the direction of Big Shanty, the first depot above Marietta on rail road. Incamped for the night Monday and formed a line of battle in reserve and threw up entrenchments. During the day we were again moved to the right a short distance and close to the rail road. We again threw up inbankments to protect us from the shell and shot of the enmey skirmishing on along our lins. Rain a much a plenty. The roads are so bad that it is with difficulty artillery can be moved.

Thursday, 9th, Again moved to the right and east of the rail road and halted in front of Kennesaw Mountain and in rear of Featherston's Brigade. The enemy shell us very heavy as we marched up the lins in full view of them. Fortunately no one of the 43d was hurt.

Friday, 10th. Skirmishing as usual along our lins and a good deal of shelling on both sids through the day. The rain still continues, rendering camp life very disagreeable. More so from the fact that we are confined to the ditches the greater portion of the time.

Saturday 11th. It is just one month to day since our corpse arrived at Resacca. We passed through a great many hardships and privations but the army is in fine spirits. The utmost confidence in General Johnson prevails throughout the entire army and I have yet to see the first man who doubts but that we will whip the hated Yankees. Skirmishing and shelling still continues with no purticular results on either side.

Sunday, 12th. All was remarkable quite today save an occassional shell from the enmys batteries. Monday, 13th. The same sound of shelling picket fireing to day as yesterday.

Tuesday the 14th, Lt. General Polk was killed while riding on our picket lins. The Army of Miss. regret his death. We looked on him as a farther. While at New Hope Church he rode up to our boys and said, "Boys, we have a long account to settle with Sherman for chaseing us through

46

Miss." He was killed with a cannon ball passing through his boddy. Gen. Hardee was standing close by. Gen. Looreing takes command of the corps and Gen. Featherston the divission.

Wendsday 15th. Cannonadeing and skirmishing the order of the day. In the eavening the enmy made a charge upon our pickets and were driven back. The 20th Miss. losted some 30 killed and wounded. Among the killed was Maj. Massy. His boddy fell into hands of the Yankies. The 40th and 31st Miss. have several wounded. Thursday 16th, The armys still continue to skirmish with each other. The enmy is reported to be moveing on our right. We rec. this day full purticulars of the Forrest victory in Miss. It rejoyest our hearts to know that our loved ones at home were again saved from the presence of the ruthless invader by intrepid and gallant Forrest and the men under his command.

Friday 17th. Heavy skirmishing and cannonadeing dureing the day and man in the 43d was killed this eavening by the explosion of a shell. Saturday 18th. Raining in torrents. Gen. Woods is moveing to the left. It is being reported that the enmy is endeavoring to flank us by way of Powder Springs. Skirmishing active in our front, at sun down commenced to fall back to a new position a mile and a half nearer Marietta. Our lins now extend east and west running over the tops of big and little Kennesaw Mountains on whose summits we have batteries planted. From the tops of these mountains we can see all the movements of the Yankees. They can not make any movement or attack our lins on any part without it being discovered and reported to our commanders. The principal shelling of the enmy so far has been directed at our batteries on these mountains. Before we fell back to them it was a great place of resort for Ladies and noncombatnants.

Sunday the 19th. Still raining. The 43d on picket for

the first time. No one hurt dureing the day. In the evening there was a cavalry fight with the enmys on our right wing which ended in their being repulsed and driven back.

Monday the 20th. This morning all is still save a few shells from enmy now and then. Late in the eavening Gen. Hardee fought the Yankees. The battle lasted some three hours. He defeated them with considerable loss.

Tuesday the 21st. Today nothing unusual has occured save the fireing of a few cannon. The enmy is making strong efforts to flank us on the left So far he has been defeated in all his plans. Wendsday, the 22d. Gen. Hardee attacked the enemy driving them from three lines of breastworks, captureing 60 prisoners and 13 peices of cannon. Sherman is making every effort to flank us on the right.

Thursday, 23, Today the same routine of shelling and skirmishing. Late in the eavening the enemy made another attack on the left of a   loss.

Friday, 24th, very little picket fireing or cannonading today. Saturday, 25th, At 10 A.M. an artillery duel between our batteries on the top the Little Kennesaw and the enemys and again at 3 P.M. The loss of the enemy on our left for the two last days is 2 Gen. officers and 1800 men, so says a deserter who came into our lines this morning.

Sunday, 26th. Beautiful Sabath morning. What a pleasure it would be to attend Ola Fellowship or North Union and worship God, away from the roar of cannon and the rattle of small arms. Skirmishing throughout the night and has been tolerable brisk all day.

Monday, 27th. Heavy cannonading and skirmishing all along our lines this morning. At 1/2 after   the enemy advanced in line of battle and drove in the pickets of Scott's   Our main   batteries   on them verry heavy. This has indeed been a day of cannonading. The shells flew all around me, but through the tender mercies of God I have been sheilded from harm. The enemy advanced on several lines of battle on Hardee and a portion of Loreing Corps and were repulsed with heavy loss. Their loss is estimated at five thousand, ours one hundred fifty. Dureing the fight the woods took fire, and a great many of the Yankee wounded were burned to death. All the prisners agree in the statement that their men were intoxicated. It seems they cannot be brought to face the music without being half drunk and the consequence is they do very bad shoots and hence our small loss.

(End of George W. Berryhill's Letter)

Chattahoochee River

Chattahoochee River, Seven Miles North of Atlanta, Ga.
Thursday, July 14th, 1864

Dear Ira,

I received your letter of the 5th inst. on yesterday. I was truly sorrow to hear that your little boy was dead, but was glad to see that you gave him up with such Christian like fortitude. "The Lord giveth and the Lord taketh away. Blessed be the name of the Lord." It is good for a man to say, "Thy will be done, oh Lord," if we can say it from the heart. Ira, I hope that you are trying to love the Lord. You have a tie in heaven now that binds you more closely than ever before, a child in heaven. And, Ira, you have a wife that professes the name of Jesus. I feel shure that you will press on hand in hand toward that heavenly home above. A praying wife is the greatest and best gift bestowed upon man.

Who can resist the prayers of a devoted wife. I feel that it was the prayers of a precious wife that caused me to seek Jesus and find him precious to my never dying soul, and I feel that it is by her prayers that I am still in the land of the living. I might say a great deal on this subject but I only have time to write a short letter and will have to say but a fiew words on a subject.

Your baby was indeed a small one, but some of those small seven months infants make the most robust children of any others. My oldest boy, for instance, was the smallest infant that I ever saw but is a perfect whale now.

I am in very good health now and am feeling stronger and better than I have for some time past. I have got well rested. The army crossed the Chattahoochee on the night of the 9th inst., since which time we have all been having a glorious resting spell. Our Corps [Stewart's] camped 4 miles from Atlanta where we remained untill 2 o'clock this morning when Adams' Brigade returned to the river to do picket duty, relieving some other Brigade that had been on for some days. I do not know what the Yanks are up to. They have made no effort to cross the river at this point. They fire an occasional cannon from our old works on the other side of the river at our batteries on this side, doing no harm that I have heard of. The Yanks appear to be very scarce over there and my opinion is that they are going in some other direction leaving just enough men behind to keep up a show and will turn up before long in some other place. But I guess that Old Jo has his eye upon the blue whelps.

George is quite sick today. I fear that he is taking the fever. He is with me and I have some bord shelters that will keep him dry if it rains. If he is not better by tomorrow he will be sent to the hospital. If you see George's wife any time soon tell her that she does not write to him as often as she ought.

You enquire about Blant Caldwell. He has just returned to his command today. He has been at hospital 2 months but not sick all the time. He was detailed as ward master in one of the hospitals at Lagrange, Ga. He is all right. I have not seen Lewis Thompson since the 19th May when he was detailed to go to the trains to cook for his Co. which he did for near 4 weeks when he was taken very sick and sent to a hospital. I do not know where and have never been able to learn. I do not know wheather he is dead or alive. If you have any information from him please write me. The Confederacy never has any better soldier than Lewis. I hope that he has been furloughed home.

    James Clegg was in hospital but returned today. A. C. McVey, D. Moore, B. F. McCain, A. Holmes, Tom Gilbert, Haze Lamb, J. E. Huffman, and Jim Randle have all been sent to hospital but I am not informed where except A. Holmes who is at Lagrange, Ga. Dock, Jimmy, Silas, Truss, Cook and Bob Cochran are all well. I have not seen Cook but once since Lewis was sent to hospital. He is cooking rations for his Co. I saw Tom Cochran yesterday. He is well but looks like myself, rather slim. I see Eugene and Tom Harvey and Capt. Middleton, Green, Davis, Dick Walpole and many other of our old acquaintances every fiew days. They are all doing well so far as I know. Marshall Rose is at Hospital sick. West is in command of his Co. Capt. Tinnon is about sick as usual. Parker has resigned and I think Tinnon will soon, so Marshall will be captain. He ought to have been long ago.

    I wrote to Mary to send me a trunk. I hope that she has not done so for I have got me an old one and patched it up and made a very good one out of it. I need nothing to it but a lock and key. I can do very well without anything in the clothing line more than I have untill fall except shoes. I am nearly barefooted and it is almost an impossibility for an officer to get shoes here. The government will not sell to an officer when there is a demand for them among the soldiers. If there are any left after the soldiers are all supplied then an officer can buy. If Tom has not returned when you get this please send me a pair. Ira, write often for you know how uneasy I am to hear from home now. I wrote you five or six days ago. I hope you have got it.

>Your Bro. and friend,
>W. H. Berryhill

Camp Near Chattahoochee River

My Dear Wife,

    I wrote to Brother   and requested him to send the letter to you as I did not expect to have an opportunity to write to you for some days. But I find that there is a gentleman going to start to Demopolis, Ala., this evening so I will write you a short letter by him and let him mail it at that place. There is such an immense amount of mail matter sent out from Atlanta that it gets badly mixed up and there are many letters that never get through.

    We crossed the Chattahoochee on the night of the 9th inst. and came out some 2 miles from the River where we have been laying around every since, doing nothing in the world. We burned the Rail Road's other bridges after evening. Our army holds the east bank and the enemy holds the west bank of the Chattahoochee.

    Sherman does not appear to push forward as he has usually done, in fact it is currently reported in camp that he is falling back, but I do not believe it though it is certain that that portion of his army that flanked us on our right and crossed the river above before we did have recrossed to the west or north side. But I do not consider this evidence sufficient to say that the whole army is falling back. I know this--that we have fallen back from position to position untill the whole army is getting heartily tired of it, and say that if the fight is ever going to come off that they want it to come soon and be done with it.

The impression now is that if the enemy crosses the River that Johnston will attack them immediately. I hope that he will but I suppose that he knows best what he ought to do. I have never seen an army better managed in retreat in my life than this has been. It has always been moved quietly and slowly just as if there was no enemy about. The army has been well fed and clothed all the while and has not become demoralized scarcely any at all. But my opinion is that if we go below Atlanta that the army will become badly demoralized for they have been told all the while that the big fight would be shure to come off when we reached the Chattahoochee. We are now to that river and across it--with the very great prospect of going below Atlanta. Everything was being run off from Atlanta untill yesterday. Gen. Johnston ordered it stopped which looks a little like Atlanta is to be held.

We have it reported here that Kirby Smith has crossed the Miss. River and is moving on Sherman's rear with Forrest. If it be so Sherman may have to fall back. The dispatches from Richmond today is that Grant is falling back and that a part   [one complete paragraph torn off here] will today, having got well rested, but am losing some flesh. I have had but very little sickness since I left Montevallo, but have went through many hardships which is the cause of my losing so much flesh. I would suppose that I am 20 lbs. less than when you saw me last. My present position is a little easier than the one that I occupied in Co. D, but even this is a laborious one. I have not got a horse to ride yet. I hope that I will have soon.

I have got nearly all my clothing except my coat. I have sent for my saddle bags several times and the quartermaster has always sent me just a portion of my clothing, leaving my saddle bags behind. I do not know wheather I will get my coat or not. They sent me my new shirt that I bought about the time I left Montevallo a fiew days ago and I have it on now for the first time. I bought an Irish linen shirt yesterday for which I am to pay $20. It is worth at least 60 or 75 dollars in the market. The linen shirt that I brought with me is good yet though I have ruined the bosom by getting it stained with dewberrys and blackberrys. The Domestick shirts that I brought with me are about gone up. The one that I have with me will wear one more week. The other I reckon is in my saddle bags.

My drawers are good, my pants are giving out. My nice janes ones are about ready for the patch and nothing to patch them with. I took them off yesterday and had them washed which is the first time that I have had them off since I left Ala. I wrote you that if you had anything like a shirt that would do me any good for you to send it by Tom, but you see as the matter now stands I am not in need of shirts or drawers. As to shoes and socks, I am about barefooted and this is a rocky country for a man to travel without shoes.

I got letter from you and Ira and John and Newt all on the 4th and 5th of July. I would much rather have got them a week later but I fear that just at the time that I want to hear from you the worst that nobody will write at all. Mary, I think of you many times every day and pray for you often. I feel that God will be with you and take care of you and our little children. Mary, I think of you at night and at morning and throughout the fatigues of the day you buoy me up and keep me from desponding. I shall never cease to love you. I send you two pieces of poetry which expresses my feelings toward you better than I can write them. I sent 2 song ballads to Laura from Montevallo. Did she get them? One was "Do They Miss Me At Home" and the other was "When This Cruel War Is Over." I hope to hear from you soon. Good bye.

                    Your Affectionate Husband

To My Wife

I am thinking of thee, dear Wife,
Of thy virtues and thy worth,
And I hear thy kind and gentle voice,
The dearest to me on earth.
I feel again the pressure,
Of thy loving tender hand,
And I long to be beside the,
In our own dear native land.

You will not forget me darling,
Though I am far away,
For I'll meet the at the dawning
Of a brighter better day.
And we'll trust in our Maker,
That the day we soon shall see,
When our flag will float above us,
All happy, proud and free.

W. H. B.

Brown's Mills

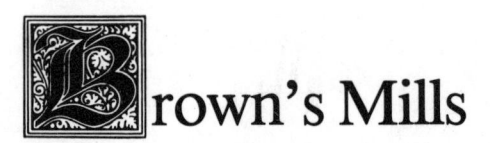

Brown's Mills, Seven Miles North of Atlanta, Ga.
Monday, July 18, 1864

My Dear Ira, John and Willie,

    I wrote to Laura yesterday but was too late for the mail so I will write a fiew lines to you this morning to let you know where I am   fight last evening. Gen. Adams prepared to fight them but Gen. Loring stopped him and ordered him to fall back across Peachtree Creek which is a half mile from where we were yesterday. Adams had a man or two killed and several wounded. I was not with the Brigade. I was ordered across the creek with the wagons and went across before the Yankees came up. I and 12 of my corps are at a large bridge for the purpose of burning it if the Yankees advance upon it. We came here at dark last night and piled up dry rails upon the bridge and under it. We had lots of pine split up and every man had a handful. We kept fire burning all night ready to light our torches and put fire to the bridge, but the Yanks have not come up yet so we have not burned the bridge and the sun is 2 hours high. Our brigade is in line of battle on the hill close to the bridge. I am well this morning. I have not heard from George.

    I want you to be good boys and do all that you can to make your Ma happy. And you shall have the love of your Dear Pa.

Browns Mills, Seven Miles from Atlanta, Ga.
Tuesday, July 19, 1864

My Dear Wife,

    I have a chance to send a letter to Starkville by a negro going there. So I avail myself of the opportunity as I never let any chance pass without writing. I have written a number of letters since I received one from you. I sent one to the children yesterday. The last that I received from you was dated the 24th June. But I heard from you up to the 4th of July by a letter from Ira. I have been expecting a letter for the last 2 days. I think that I will get one this morning.

    I am well and have the most devouring appetite that I ever had. I eat too much sometimes which causes me to have severe heartburn at times. I suppose that I am a little Dis-peptic. I have had but little sickness since I left home, but I have got to be very lean and poor. I only weigh 145 lbs. I am not so strong when I am poor this way, but I feel better than I did when I was so fat.

    George was sent to the division hospital at Atlanta about a week ago. I thought when he started to the hospital that he was taking a fever, but I reckon that it was only cold. I heard from him yesterday. He was about well except his back. He is bad off with that.

    We thought this morning that there would be a battle today but up to this hour, 12 o'clock, I see no more sign of it than there was yesterday. Adams' brigade had like to have gotten into a fight Sunday evening and I expect would if Gen. Loring had not come up just in time to stop Gen. Adams, who then fell back across Peachtree Creek at Brown or Moors Mill [I forgot which]. It is a large creek and had a long bridge on it but I burned it up last night. Our men hold our side of the creek and the enemy the other.

    Gen. Johnston has been relieved from the command of the Army of Tennessee by order of the President. It has cast a gloom over the whole army so far as I have been able to hear it spoken of. He was well beliked in this army. I do not know his offense. Gen. Hood is in command.

Mary, I want to hear from you very bad.[1] You must write often and have Laura to write. I must close this letter soon for I have just got orders to be ready to march at a moment's warning. I expected to write a long letter when I began. I think that we are going to fall back to near Atlanta. Capt. Gilbert is sick but is still with the regt. I hope that it is only cold that is the matter with him.

I have got me a trunk. I hope that you have not sent me yours. I have got all my clothing and bedding from the baggage wagon except my coverlet. I am needing shoes very bad and a bad prospect to get them here. Send me some if you can. I must close. I am yours while life lasts,

W. H. Berryhill

---

1. W. H. Berryhill knew that Mary was expecting their seventh child in July (Mary Lula was actually born on July 17, 1864). His letter of June 5, 1864, spoke of it first, when he said, "I would almost give my life to be at home with you for the next six weeks . . . ." From then until August his concern for his wife is obvious, although he never mentions her condition by name.

Atlanta

July and August, 1864
Near Atlanta, Ga.

This company since last mustered has continued with the Army of Tennessee, performing its prorata share of picket and skirmish duty during the retreat, from Kennesaw Mountain to this place, a distance of 25 miles.

Atlanta, Ga., Monday night, July 25th, 1864

My Verry Dear Wife,

    Through the mercy of an all wise Maker I am still alive and permitted to write another letter to you, but I do not know that it will ever reach you. I expect to send this out by a negro who is going to try to go to Mississippi. I wrote you a letter last Tuesday, the 19th inst. to be sent out by a negro. I don't think he started. We found that the Montgomery R. Rd. was cut by the Yankees so that   was cut off and the negro did not go. I only have a short time to write to you tonight for I will have to go to work at Midnight and it is after 10 o'clock. I have worked a portion of nearly every night for the last 2 weeks and sometimes all night.

    I have been in good health all the time. I sent the letter of the 19th by mail but I have no idea that it ever went. We fell back to the Chattachoochee River on Sunday, the 17th. We crossed Peachtree Creek and formed a line of battle on the hills south of the creek. On Monday night I with my corps burned a large bridge on the creek to keep the Yankess from crossing, but on the next day, Tuesday the 19th, the enemy crossed the creek above the mill and in the evening Reynold's Brigade and the 15th Miss. of our brigade made an attack upon them. The 15th made a gallant charge driving the Yankees before them and in to the creek, capturing and bringing off 52 prisoners. Some 200 or more surrendered to them but not being supported by Reynolds they all made their escape but the 52. We lost a good many men, but I have not had an opportunity to get a list of them. Eugene Harvey was killed, Medy Oswalt missing and supposed killed.

    The next evening there was a heavy charge made upon the right of us. Featherston's Brigade was in it and got badly cut up. Col. Drane badly wounded, Capt. Thornton wounded, supposed to be mortally. Lt. Wormack wounded. In one regt. all the captains were killed or wounded but one, and he was on picket. Lieut. West of the 33d [Tinnons Co.] was killed. Marion Spencer missing. The fight took place two miles to the right of where our brigade was in line. Adams marched up to the scene of action but got in about the close of the fight and did not get to fire a gun. I understand that one of the Tharp boys were killed but do not know which.

    George is at Macon, Ga., in the hospital. I got a letter from him yesterday. He is well except rheumatism in his feet. Capt. Gilbert, J. W. E. Spencer and the boys are all well.

Billy

Atlanta, Ga., Tuesday evening, July 26th, 1864

My Dear Wife,

    I wrote to you late last night to be sent off today. I do not know that it has gone. I think that I will have a chance to send by a man that is to start tomorrow so I write again. I am seeing a hard time of it just now. I closed your letter at about midnight and then went to where my men were at work and remained untill nearly day. I was very sleepy while I wrote which accounts in part for the bad spelling and composition.

    I have been on duty a portion of nearly every night for the last two weeks. I have been engaged in ditching on the picket line since breakfast this morning until an hour before sunset. I am pretty tired but not too much so to write you a short note. I am in very good health. If I had not been I never could have stood up under the hardships that I have gone through.

We came in to the fortifications around Atlanta on Thursday the 21st inst. On Friday the 22d Hardee attacked the enemy on our right and whipped them pretty badly, capturing some 3000 prisoners and 25 or 30 pieces of artillery. I do not know what our loss is. It is said to be small, but I think under all the circumstances that it must be heavy. Maj. Gen. Walker of Ga. was killed, 3 Yankee Generals were killed and one wounded. Among the killed was Gen. McPherson. He is equal to Sherman.

Loring's Division charged the enemy out four miles north of Atlanta the day before we came here and Featherston's brigade got badly cut up. I gave you the names of those that I could recollect in the letter that I wrote last night and will not try to give any in this. I will send a list of all the killed and wounded in the Choctaw Cos. as soon as I can get the time to get it up. Send Mrs. Snow word that Bud was not in the fight but is in the hospital sick, but I don't know how bad. Our brigade was not in the fight. They were down at a Crossing place on Peachtree Creek 8 miles below to keep the Yanks from crossing there. I burned the bridge two nights before.

Mary, there are so many things taking place here every day that I get it confused and cannot state them correctly unless I could write every day. So I will not undertake to tell you much about it. I believe that you will be glad enough to hear that I am alive and well. How glad it would make me to hear from you and to hear that you are alive and doing well. I have not heard from you since the 4th of July and have got no letter from you since the one that you wrote on the 24th of June. But I do not blame you about it for the Yanks have cut off our communication and have cut the rail road between here and Montgomery. I learn that they have left there now and I hope that matters will be put in motion again soon so that we can hear from loved ones at home "sweet home."

I wish I was there. I know that you are uneasy for me,

but I hope you will let your fears pass away for God has all ways taken care of me. You can form some idea of how bad I want to hear from you by your own feeling for my safety and I want to see you and the children so bad. I will have so much to tell you of. Every one here has a hard time, so I do not think that I ought to grumble for I have a better time than some others that I see. I have been treated very well by the officers, from Gen. Adams down. I get along very well with the men of my corps and they treat me with respect. My corps has been armed and will occupy a place in the trenches if we should be charged. I am very well pleased with it for I have thought that we ought to have guns to defend ourselves with in case we were attacked at any time.

Mary, I have been in the worst tite for shoes that I ever was before, but I have a brand new pair now. I had a good shoe maker in my Co. so I got some sole leather gave to me and he took my boot legs and made me a real nice pair, so I step around as light today as you please. They only cost me $1.75 and will last me untill bad weather sets in this fall. It is better to be lucky than rich. You see that I wore my boots some 10 months and then for $1.75 I got a pair of shoes out of them that will last me 3 or 4 months more.

We have the strangest fortifications here than we have had any where that I have been and I do not now think that Atlanta will be given up without we are whipped out of it, and I do not [think] that will be the case. I wish that I could have heard from you just one more time before the R.R. was cut. It was just the time I wanted to hear from you the worst. May God care for you and our little ones.

Your Billy

Atlanta, Ga., Sunday, July 31st, 1864

My Dear Wife,

    I wrote you two days ago, in fact I have wrote you every two or three days for the last ten days. Frank Holloway told me a little while ago that if I would get a letter to him this evening that he knew of a chance to get it off to Choctaw for me. I do not know who by nor I do not care so I get the letter off to you. If I knew that all the letters that I have written went safe to you I would write to someone else, but I do not know that they do so I direct all to you, for I know that you feel more interest in me than all the world besides.

    Everything has been quiett since the bloody little fight of last Thursday, at least it has been so right about Atlanta. But a raid has passed to our rear cutting the Macon R.R. and capturing all or nearly all of our QuarterMasters and their trains with all fine teams and many fine horses belonging to Gens. and their Aides, Cols, Majs and c. with all their fine clothing and baggage of every discription, belonging to men and officers from Lieuts up to Gen. I lost nothing but my coverlet, Hardee's Tactics and Army regulations. Jimmy Spencer lost his valice containing a part of his clothing and all of the company papers and some blankets. Dock lost his saddle bags with a piece or two of clothing and a quilt. The Yankees burned the wagons and carried off the mules and horses. There was some four or five hundred wagons and at least 2,000 mules and horses. They captured nearly all quarter masters with their clearks, teamsters, and c., amounting to some 400 or 500 men, unless more of them escaped than I have heard of. They captured Gen. Loring's fine horse. He was very much like a horse that I used to have that I called Paddy. Gen. Featherston said that he would not have taken $10,000 for his trunk. I saw a Sutler who made his escape. He says that his loss is $10,000. It was a perfect smash up shure, and I have no idea that a half a million of dollars will replace it.

Jackson's caverly was down there [it was some 25 miles below here] and did not know that the Yankees were about untill they had burned the trains and were tearing up the R.R. They are in pursuit of them but they are so worthless that no one expects anything to be done. Mary, a heavy rain is beginning to fall and I have no shelter. I will stop till it is over.

Mary, I learn since writing the above that David L. Sweatman will carry this letter. Brantly is promoted to Brigadier Gen. and Davy is on his staff. I met Brantly the other day while we were getting into position for fight. He had got his papers but a fiew hours before. I got a letter from George 2 days ago. He is at Columbus, Ga. and has rheumatism but is able to walk about. It distresses me very bad that I can get no letter from home. You must write by Sweatman when he returns. Still continue to pray for your husband.

W. H. Berryhill

Atlanta, Ga., Monday, August 1st, 1864

Dear Brother,

I learn that Lieut. Parker will start home tomorrow and I take the opportunity to write you a short letter to let you know that I am still in the land of the living and in the enjoyment of tolerable good health. I have not heard or received a word from you since your letter of the 21st June and I have heard nothing of my family since the 4th of July. You know the condition of my family so I need not tell you that I am suffering great anxiety on their account. We have had no mails here for more than 2 weeks on account of the R.R. being cut. Every R.R. to this place has been cut. The one leading to Macon was the last which was just 3 or 4 days ago cut by a raid that captured and destroyed all our QM trains with all the QM's and their clerks, teamsters, and c.

The wagons were burned with all the baggage [belonging to officers principally] except what they did   them. The train was some 25 miles   Macon R.R. and numbered some   time to damage the road much before our caverly got after them. The road is in operation again. It was only stopped about 48 hours.

Jackson's Caverly was guarding down in that country and let them in right under their noses, but they went in hot fast after them and we learned last night and this morning that the Yankees attacked a train loaded with troops when the cars stopped and let the troops out upon them, and they drove the Yanks back three miles, when Jackson came up in their rear and scattered them to the 4 winds capturing a large number of them and are still picking them up out of the woods. I learn that we recaptured the greater part of the mules.

Another raiding party of 1100 were captured yesterday at Nunan station with 3 pieces of Artillery and their trains and c. I am told that this was done by Gen. Ruddy who was coming to reinforce this army and happened to be in the right place to take them on surprise. The troops here were very much disheartened on account of these raids untill they have begun to take them in out of the wet.

Newt, I am obliged to   . I have written many letters to Mary in the last 10 days   will please carry her this one and read those that   news. I wrote her by D. L. Sweatman   been quiett in front since last Thursday.   all well except J. W. E. Spencer who   . George is in hospital at Columbus, Ga.

W. H. Berryhill

P.S. I do not know that I gave you the correct acts of these raiding parties. I give it as I get it. But I am shure that we are using them up badly. The Yanks cannot fight us out of Atlanta, but I am inclined to think that they will maneuver us out. We are well fortified. WHB

Atlanta, Ga., Wednesday, Aug. 3rd, 1864

My Dear Son,

I received your nice little letter last night. It made me verry proud to see that you could write so well and proves to me that you are taking my advice and trying to learn to read and write as fast as you can. I also got a letter from your grandma Berryhill who stated that you were a good boy and was very obedient to mind everything that she told you. These things made me very proud of you, my boy, and hope that you will continue to act as you have began untill you get to be a man and then you will be respected by all.

[One fold of letter torn off here, losing two paragraphs]

The mail came in last night for the first time in a long time. I got six letters, viz. one from your Ma and Laura in the same envelope, one from you, one from Uncle Frank, one from Mother, and one from Newton. I expected to get more letters by Tom this morning as I had heard of him and Zack on the way so I went to the Regt. this morning. But was surprised to learn that they had been turned back by a busy scoundrel after they had got within a days travel of here. This rascal was no one else than Owens Gore. I learn that he told them to go back home and told them that Loring's Division was cut all to pieces and were all killed, captured and scattered to the winds. If we had the puppy here we would maul him.

Atlanta, Ga., Friday, August 5th, 1864

My Dear Wife,

I received your letter of the 18th July two or three days ago. You have no idea how much it relieved my anxiety. It was after supper when I got the letter and it made me so glad to hear that you had come through so well and safe that it was late at night before I could compose myself enough to sleep. I had prayed very often for this and when I found that it was as I had asked for it to be, I felt much rejoiced and thankful that there is a prayer hearing and a prayer answering God.

Mary, our prayers are not always answered because we sometimes ask amiss. Not that we ask for things that God cannot give or is not willing to give, but we ask in our own will and do not feel resigned to let God's will be done. For instance, when you pray to God to spare my life and bring me safely home again, do you feel in your heart that you are entirely willing that the Lord's will may be done. And if I should be taken from the earth that you could say amen, "Thy will be done O Lord, on earth as it is in heaven." If I fall in this war far from those that love me so well God's will be done for me. When a battle is raging and men are falling by hundreds do you believe that God sees them all individually. He most certainly does for he has said that not a sparrow falleth without his knowledge. Then, Mary, I cannot fall without God's knowledge for shurly I am worth as much as a sparrow. And if I live faithful here on earth I shall live again in Heaven.

At the time I got yours and Laura's letters [which were in the same] I got 4 others, viz. I from Newt, I from Mother, I from Uncle Frank and one from Buddy. I answered Bud's letter the next day and gave it to Old Hubbard Conner to carry out to Miss. to be mailed. I told Buddy to carry his letter to you and that I would write to all of you at the same time for you could read each other's letters and hear from me the oftener. I have learned since I saw Mr. Conner that he did not get off as he expected, so I write this letter sooner than I otherwise would have done and it may reach you before Ira's letter.

I was verry much surprised to see how well Ira could write. I hope that Newt will keep him at it untill he writes a good hand. Tell Laura that I will write to her before long. She may look for the next letter.

You stated that you would write again by Tom, but he did not get here. Him and Zack got within a day's travel of here and got scared off of the track and turned back. One of the Rasberry boys saw them when they were starting back and they told him that Owens Gore told them that it was no use to go any further for our Brigade was all cut up and scattered. Owens has since come up here and denies the most of it and says that he did not know what to advise them to do and gave them a pass to go home. He says that he did not know that he was coming up here or he would have brought them on with him. I think that Zack and Tom was anxious to get some excuse to go back and was glad to get hold of any rumor that would justify them to turn back, and I know that Owens is bad to exagerate. I think that the best thing that could be done for Tom and Zack would be to give them 200 lashes apiece.

I learn that Tom had my trunk. I am sorrow that it was sent for I have got one here and if Tom brings it back do not send it again. I do not know that you were sending anything to me in the trunk, but expect that there was shoes as I wrote for them when I did for the trunk. I have procured shoes. Socks and pants will be the first thing that I shall need and by a little patching I can make my pants do me untill cold weather.

I have no news to write you. Our position is 2 miles west of Atlanta. The Yankees are close in our front and there is heavy picket fighting every day. I am having but little to do now and have managed to keep a plenty to eat though rations are somewhat reduced since the Raiders cut the R.R. Those raiders have nearly all been captured. Be shure to write by first mail after you get this.

Yours as ever,
W. H. Berryhill

Atlanta, Ga., Friday, August 12th, 1864

Dear Ira,

    I received your letter day before yesterday dated July 22d. The last that I received before this one was dated July 5th. I mention this to show you that I do not get all the letters that you write for your last says that you write once or twice per week. Speaking of this reminds me of a thing that I have been wanting to enquire about for a long time but would always forget it when writing, viz. how many mails do you have per week from Starksville and on what days do they come to Greensboro. I wish to know this so as I may govern myself in writing here to suit the mail there.

    Ira, I have nothing in the world to write you that will be of interest to you, and I know that you always expect something of interest when you get a letter from the army. The knowledge of this always embarrasses me in writing when I have nothing to write. I am well and doing as well as you can expect a man to do under these circumstances.

    The Yankees are in gun shot of us and at their old trade ditching up to us. But in some places we are advancing on them by ditching. They want to play Vicksburg on us if they could, but they can't quite come it for we have a plenty of good cannon and gunners that are not afraid to fire on them whenever it suits them. The Yanks are beginning to find that Jordan is a hard road to travel after all.

We have powerful works here and are still improving them every day. We are fixing for a regular siege and the Yankees appear to be fixing themselves to besiege us in regular style. I think that we can hold them at bay for sometime to come. Their raids to our rear have been so badly used up that I think that they will be very cautious how they make them in the future.

Gen. Wheeler has gone to the enemies' rear with two divisions of caverly. It is reported here that he captured Marietta day before yesterday, with all of their supplies there with their supply trains. It is also reported that Wheeler was killed at or near Marietta. Some prisoners have arrived here which are said to have come from Marietta. It is further reported that Tunnel Hill has been blown up which blocks the R.R. Now if all these reports be true the Yankees will be in a slim fix for rations soon. It is said that it was Buford that blew up the tunnel. But I had supposed that Buford was still with Forrest in Miss.

Our army are beginning to show some signs of demoralization and I hear of desertions occasionally. But I do not suppose that an army has ever stood up better than this. Gen. Johnston is still the favourite of this army and could lead them farther than any man living. Hood is a great Gen. but he cannot manage to keep up the spirit of the army as Johnston did. We have had news from Mobile and if that falls it will operate very much against us here. But you can hear more of Mobile than I can so I will not write of it.

I wrote to Laura a fiew days ago that I expected that Frank McCain was dead, but he arrived here today looking better than usual. Arch Holmes came in 2 days ago, not very stout. Lewis Thompson came in last week. He is tolerable well. George, Dock, Jimmy, Silas, Bob O. Cook and all the rest of the boys that are present are well.

Give my compliments to Capt. Thompson and tell him to write to me when convenient. Is Proctor still on my place. Blant Caldwell is a candidate for Treasurer. Who are in the field there. How do you think that George will run for assessor. I do not know how I would vote if I was there, but my notion is that T.B.T. would make a good Probate Judge and would suit you better if you remain Clerk than any one else, but I suppose that I am too far off to form conclusions.[1]

Write again soon. Send this letter to Mary. The mails are running regular now.

Your Brother and Friend,
W. H. Berryhill

---

1. Ira McDowell served as Probate Clerk from 1862-1870. According to a list included in *Choctaw County Chronicles* by J. P. Coleman, T. N. Davis was elected Probate Judge for this term.

Atlanta Ga Wednesday Aug 17th 1864
My Dear Wife
As Allen Moore is here & is going out to morrow morning I avail myself of the opportunity to write you. I have nothing of interest to say to you only that I am well. I would have been glad to have got a letter from you by Uncle Allen Moor but I presume that you did not know that he was coming, he & Bill Thompson arived here day before yesterday. Uncle Allen brought me letters from Newt & Ira J, which stated that you were all well. Ira's letter tells me a different story from you & Laura about the looks of the babe he says that it is the prettiest little fellow that I ever saw, he wrote me that Lizzie had been sick. I was sorrow to hear it. He says that Newton tells him that he is learning very fast. He tells me that you have had a hard storm there the night before he wrote this has been a bad year for rains & storms. He says that his Grand Pa McMade forty bushels of wheat that was more than it looked like it could make when I left home, I believe that

I will have to depend upon Ira J. entirely for news from home, for this is the second letter that I have got from him since I have got one from you or Laura. I am glad to see him inclined to write & will answer him every time that he writes. I have answered both of his letters. Newton's Letter brings me the glad tidings of Laura's conversion. Mary I feel under renewed obligation to God to continue to pray for mercy & blessings. I feel now that God hears me when I pray & I feel too that he is a prayer hearing & a prayer answering God. I pray God to lead her on in the ways of peace of holiness and that she may be instrumental in the conversion of all her brothers & sisters as they grow up to learn that Jesus died for them. Mary let us never cease to pray. We have preaching in our brigade every day or two now. I was over at the —— to preaching last night I did not know the preacher but he preached a good Sermon & after preaching he call for mourners when about 5 presented themselves. I hope that good may result from these meetings & that many may be converted to God,

I have received no letter from you since your & Laura's which was dated a month ago to day & to morrow, I suppose that you have heard of the R.R. having been cut & have concluded not to write untill you know that the mail is going again, it was only stoped a few days. I knew that the Road was cut but I did not stop writing. I do not know wheather you got my letters or not. I want to hear from you verry much. I want to know what you have called our little baba & how it is getting on. It is a hard case that I have a daughter that I have never seen & can not be permitted to go to see her.

Tell Uncle Frank & Aunt Polly that I have not seen nor heard from Newton since I got Uncles letter give them my love & compliments. The cavelry have nearly all gone to Shermans rear and Newton may be gone with them, though I am inclined to think that his command is watching the R.C.R.D. below here. Report says that Wheeler is playing the wild with old Shermans transportation, It says that he

IV

has captured Marietta with the supplies there & that he has distroyed the Rail road for twenty miles, & burned the Ettawa bridge & captured Seven trains # & burned loaded with supplies for Shermans army If this should all be true Sherman will have to get up & dust from here before many days, I have no doubt but what the report of Wheelers operations are exagera -ted but I feel shure that he is doing some -thing up there that is disturbing the yanks very much They have been very silent in our front for the last 3 days Our canons have been playing on them a good deel for three days past & theirs very seldom ever reply which is an uncommon thing for them. Our Generals have been expecting an attack ever day for a week past but still it does not come I am of opinion that they are mak -ing an effort to flank us on the left & take possession of the R.l Rd, below Atlanta They made a demonstration in that quarter a few days ago but found our troops in their front. They then move back towards our right. And a portion of our troops moved up opisite to our center & remained over there 2½ days which was up to yesterday evening when they were ordered back to our left as the enemy had re appeared there, I was at work with my corps on some Redoubts about a mile in rear of our present line. And I with all the other Pioneer Corps' were ordered to the left to do some worke near East Point some seven miles down the Rail Road Lt Williamson went with the corps down there yesterday evening & I expect to go down there to morrow I do not know how long we will have to stay down there I have my sergt, Com Commisary, Cooks, & Wagoner with me at Camps, If the Gen will let me I will carry the wagon & all hands with me To when our work is. My men carried their guns with them but I learn this morning that by the cook who carried the rations down to the men this morning, that the guns were all turned over to some one

at East Point I am glad of it if they will only keep them, for men can not manage spades & guns too.
I am well & think that I am gaining some flesh. I have been very lean. About the time that I left Montavello my hair had grown out thicker on my head than it had been for 10 years, but it has been falling off for the last three weeks untill it is thinner than it ever was before & if it continues a month longer my head will be as slick as a "pealed onion". I kep my beard shaved off except my lip & there I have a mustach which nearly hids my mouth. I bought me a shirt last week it is a striped one called hickory stripe. I have enough shirts now to last me through the winter if I do not lose any of them. my striped shirt only cost $25. I got it from the government. I have mended up my pants I can make out on them untill christmas. I will need nothing untill then but socks. Write to me soon & often. May God Bless you, Yours as ever
W H Berryhil

Atlanta, Ga., Wednesday evening, Aug. 24th, 1864

My Dear Wife,

    I wrote to you day before yesterday and sent it out by hand to be mailed on the Rl. Rd. in Miss. but I do not know that you will ever get it. I would not write again so soon but Capt. Prewitt told me yesterday that he had sent up papers to have Mr. Martin discharged and that his papers would be back in two or three days. As Mr. Martin lives in a mile or two of you, I feel shure that you will get it. I will not write again soon if I do not get a letter from you unless I have a chance to send by hand, for I have not received but the one letter from you since our babe was born, which letter was dated the 18th July, five weeks ago last Monday. I feel shure that you write but from some cause or other your letters do not reach me, and if your letters will not come here of course mine do not reach you. So it is no use for me to write. I have no knowledge of your having received a letter from me since my letter of the 7th July, and written before we crossed the Chattahoochee. In the pack of letters that Tom mailed at Montgomery there was none ever reached me from you, but I got [letters] from Newt and others and I have got letters from Ira, Newt, and Ira J. since then, and others have got letters since then and I cannot find out wheather Tom had anything for me or not. All the letters are perfectly silent on my case. I have heard of Tom's arrival at home and heard that he sold clothing to pay his expenses back, but do not know that I had anything along for him to sell.

    George is needing Tom worse now than he has ever before. He is detailed to cook for his Co. and it works him nearly to death to get through with it, but if he had Tom he could have a fine time of it and be out of harm's way. I saw George this evening. He is well. He brought me in two nice apples which was a treat to me. Common apples sell here at 2½c apiece.

I am well and gaining some flesh. Co. D is all well that is present, and numbers about [30] thirty men and have not had a man hurt yet which is more [I think] than any other Co. in the regt. can say.

My Corps has been working by the day for the last two weeks, but not at night, and we have work that will keep us for another week to come. I am doing finely for we have a regular job of work to do and some days I do not go out at all. I and Lieut. Williamson take it time about. We worked 4 days last week below East Point, some six miles south of here. Lieut. Williamson stayed down there with the men. I went down twice but only rode down and looked around awhile and then came back to camps.

We are not exposed much to shot and shell now for we are working a half mile or more in rear of our lines. The Yanks have not fired so much as are in the habit of doing since about the middle of last week, though they have shelled pretty rapidly several times today. It is generally believed that they will fight or fall back in the next five or six days. It is too dark to write more now. I will write tomorrow.

Thursday, August 25th, 1864

My Dear Wife,

It got too dark for me to finish my letter yesterday evening. So I will write more today. I have not been out to work today but have been engaged in dying some of my clothes. I used chestnut bark with a little copperas in it. I dyed one pr. of drawers and two shirts, one an old one and the other I got about the time I left Montevallo, but have only worn it two or three times and I do not wear a shirt more than a week at a time without washing if I have another to put on. I also dyed my Roundabout coat which looks very nice. In fact, it all does finely except my old shirt which I had dyed first. It is too dark. Mary, if this war keeps on long enough I will learn to do a great many things that I never knew before, and may be of some service to you after all. Mary, you need not laugh at the idea of my sweating over the dye pot for there is no telling what a man can do untill he trys. I will not colour my linen bosom shirt and my new Irish linen shirt, nor my hickory stripe shirt. You see, I have five shirts on hand.

Mary, I have just got a chance to send this letter out to Selma, Ala. by hand and I will do so for fear that Martin does not go soon. If he does get off I will write again by him. I will have to make this letter shorter than I intended to for my man cannot wait for me to make a long talk and I have delayed writing until dark and I have but one pine knot to make a light to write by.

It is reported tonight that Sherman is beginning to retreat tonight. I hope to goodness that it is so. But we may be mistaken and he may have more supplies on hand than we are aware of. Gen. Wheeler has played the very wild with Sherman's rear. He has torn the Rl. Rd. all to smash and captured Resaca and Dalton. It is said that the road can not be repaired in a month. We cannot see how Gen. Sherman can subsist his army here now without the use of the Rl. Rd. to bring his supplies down.

This strong hope that the enemy will have to leave us on account of supplies may have led us to think that the Yanks are on a retreat or preparing for it, when it is really not the case and much hard fighting may have to be done yet before this campaign is over. Gen. Hood is expecting something of the sort and it is plainly to be seen that he is making preparation for pursuit.

Mary, I cannot write the half that I intended to say this time. Do write to me often if you please, my Dear Wife. You cannot tell how bad I want to hear from you. I send some little pieces of Isinglass to the children. They have never seen any of it. This whole country is full of it and when we dig a ditch and there comes a washing rain on it the ground sparkles in every direction when the sun comes out.

Your Husband,
W. H. Berryhill

Dear children, I know that your responsibilities and cares are very great. The more I think of it the greater I feel the responsibility and the less competent I feel for the task. Mary, I sympathise with you for yours is a double task. I wish I was there to help you, but even then we would fall far short of making our children what they ought to be.

I have but little news and I reckon you are tired of it any way, but little of interest has taken place since Allen Moore left us. Only that the Yanks made a raid around us, cutting the Rl. Rd. in our rear but our caverly fought them so fast that they did it but little damage stopping the cars only some 36 hours. Our forces killed and captured some 150 or 200 of them. Our caverly force is not so strong here now as it has been, for Wheeler has gone to Sherman's rear with a very strong force. We learn today that he has captured Dalton and blown up Tunnel Hill and gone in the direction of Chattanooga.

I can write no more now for a man is waiting for this letter.

Yours affectionately,
W. H. Berryhill

You must excuse my writing on such paper for it is a scarce article here.

Your Billy

THE GENTLE REBEL *April—May, 1864*

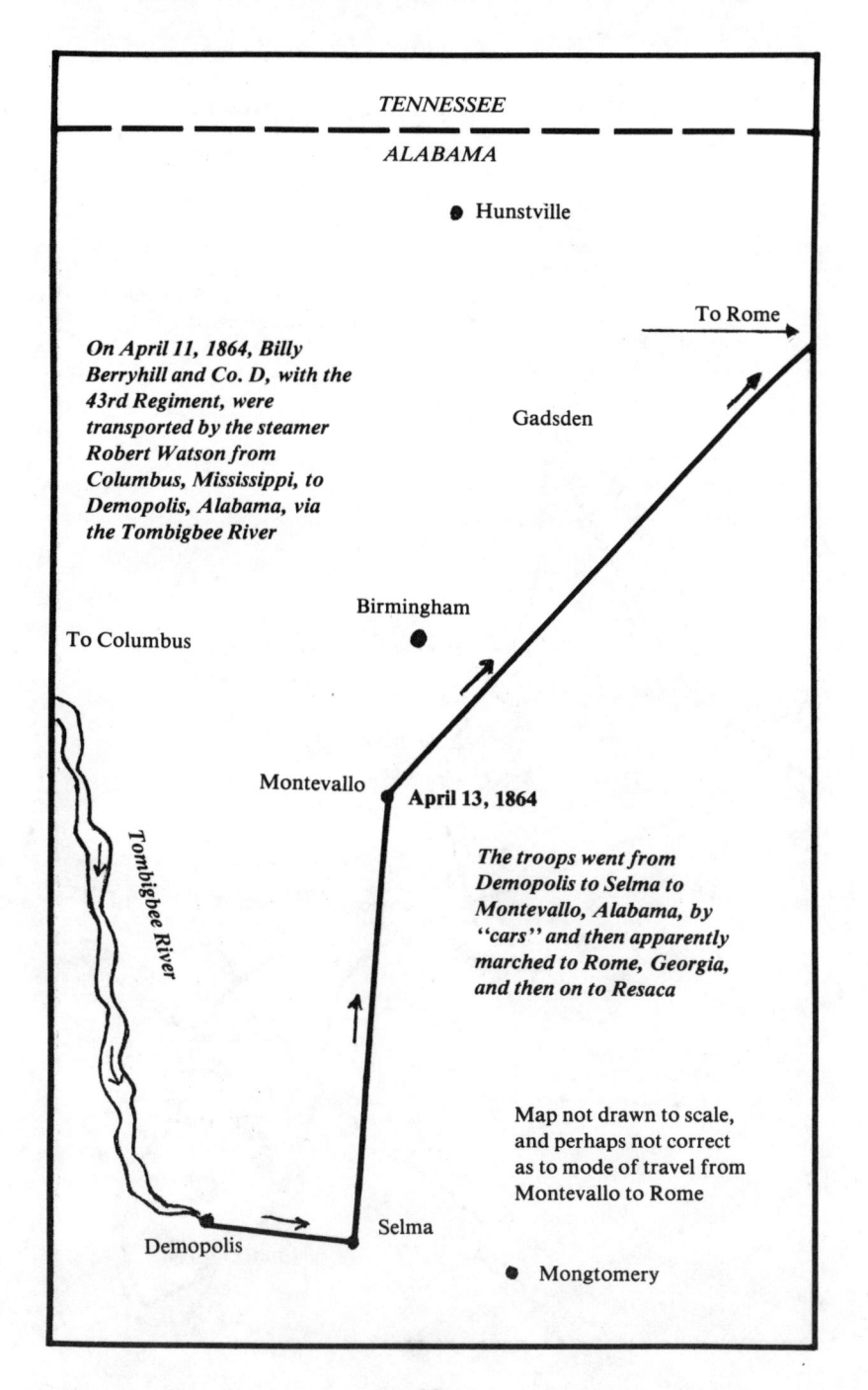

TENNESSEE
ALABAMA

● Hunstville

To Rome

On April 11, 1864, Billy Berryhill and Co. D, with the 43rd Regiment, were transported by the steamer Robert Watson from Columbus, Mississippi, to Demopolis, Alabama, via the Tombigbee River

Gadsden

To Columbus

Birmingham
●

Montevallo
● **April 13, 1864**

Tombigbee River

The troops went from Demopolis to Selma to Montevallo, Alabama, by "cars" and then apparently marched to Rome, Georgia, and then on to Resaca

Map not drawn to scale, and perhaps not correct as to mode of travel from Montevallo to Rome

Selma
Demopolis

● Mongtomery

83

Sherman's Drive to Atlanta

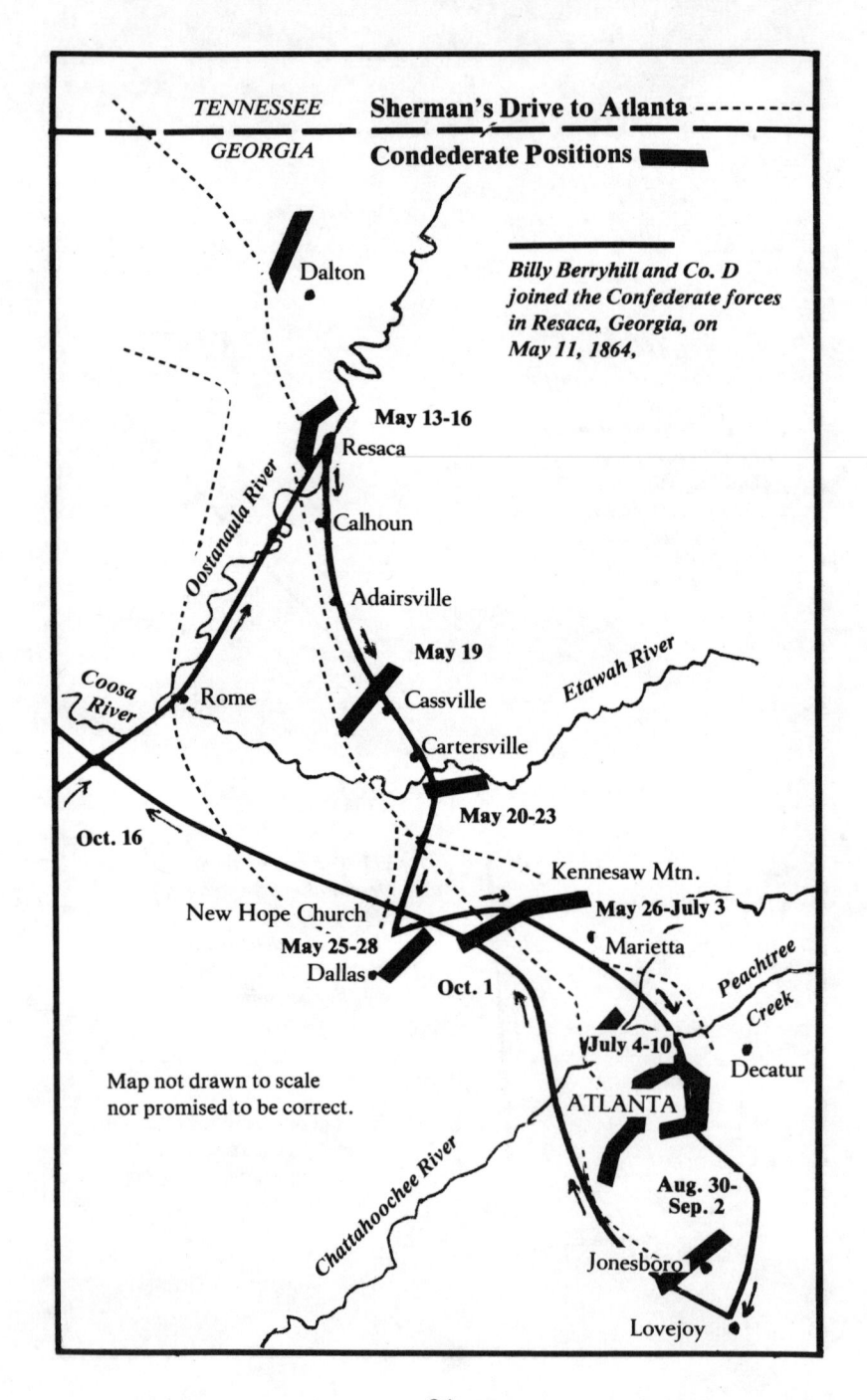

Confederate Positions

Billy Berryhill and Co. D joined the Confederate forces in Resaca, Georgia, on May 11, 1864,

- Dalton
- Resaca — May 13-16
- Calhoun
- Adairsville
- Cassville — May 19
- Cartersville — May 20-23
- Rome
- Oct. 16
- Kennesaw Mtn.
- New Hope Church
- Dallas — May 25-28
- Oct. 1
- Marietta — May 26-July 3
- Decatur
- ATLANTA — July 4-10
- Jonesboro — Aug. 30-Sep. 2
- Lovejoy

Oostanaula River, Coosa River, Etawah River, Peachtree Creek, Chattahoochee River

TENNESSEE / GEORGIA

Map not drawn to scale nor promised to be correct.

North from Atlanta

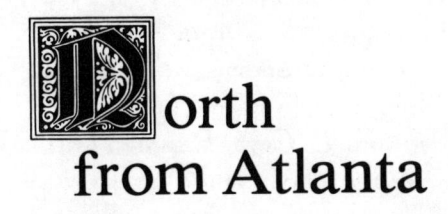

(NOTE: There was no beginning to this letter. This is a four-page folder numbered 5, 6, 7, 8.)

Capt. Randle is a clever, agreeable gentleman and being in command takes the responsibility off of me.[1] And Lieut. Fry is a splendid fellow. He is from Ala. Capt. Randle is from Miss. I am getting to be as stout and as tuff as whale bone. There is nothing that hurts me much now. I have been resting all day today. Capt. Randle and Lt. Fry are off with the Corps, cutting roads for the troops to pass along the lines. I will have to go out after a little while to take my turn at work, but I will finish this letter tomorrow and send it out by first chance as mail matters are suspended for the present.

It is strange that I never get a letter from you. I have got none yet since the one you wrote me the day after the birth of our last babe. I have no idea why it is so. I can not think that you are wilfully neglecting me.

Col. Farrell of the 15th Miss. is dead. He died a fiew days ago from sickness. I will write you more tomorrow.

1. W. H. Berryhill was in command of the Pioneer Corps of Adams Brigade from June 21, 1864, until sometime between August 25 and this letter, at which time the brigade corps had been broken up. According to information in his obituary written by his brother, S. Newton Berryhill, W. H. Berryhill was made second in command of Loring's Division Pioneer Corps, under Capt. Randle.

Camps 2 miles West of Bear Creek Station
Tuesday, Sept. 6th, 1864

My Dear Wife,

    I commenced this letter on day before yesterday and told you that I would finish it yesterday, but I was too busy yesterday to do anything at it. This is a perfect wilderness country where it is not in cultivation and troops can get about no where untill roads are cut. So you see that we are kept busy cutting roads in every direction that there is any probability that one will be needed. Our corps numbers 48 aggregate. We are now some 4 miles south of where I commenced this letter. We opened a road from the lines up there to this place. I suppose that it is designed to continue the lines down to this point. We are in camp resting and waiting for orders. I can rest very fast when I am away from the troops in a quiett place like this.

    Skirmishing was pretty heavy yesterday evening and last night, but today all is quiett. I have seen no one from the lines today. I do not know what is up.

    Mary, Tom arrived here yesterday morning bringing me 4 letters, viz. 1 from Laura, 1 from Emma, 1 from Appalona Snow, and one from Newt. But strange to tell there was none from you and Tom nor no one else could give me any reason why. Mary, I am at a loss to understand why it is that I do not get letters from you. Do you write or not. But what is the use for me to ask the question if it cannot be answered. If your letters cannot come to me please tell some one to write me why it is so. I learn from others that Tom started with clothes for me on his first trip but sold them. I would have been glad to have got a statement of the facts from you. I did not speak but a fiew words to Tom. I would rather have nocked his head off.

    George had been at my camp sick for 2 days before Tom came and I carried him up to the ambulance train yesterday morning to send him to the hospital, and while I was looking up the Surgeon I learned that Tom was at the 43d Regt. so I went and got him and carried him where George was and he carried him off to the hospital with him. Tom brought George some flour. I got some of it and we had some fresh pork on hand so we had pork and dumplins for dinner.

George was down with his back and kidneys and c. I do not think that there was anything serious the matter. I am well. I wrote you Sunday that Col. Farrell was dead. It is a mistake. I have the paper that it was said that his death was mentioned in and his name is in the list of the sick instead of the dead.

Mary, a curier has just come to us with orders for us to report back to the division as soon as possible. He informs us that the Yankees are falling back in the direction of Atlanta. I expect that they will go back in to the Atlanta fortification and rest and recruit their army there. I presume that we are going to follow them up by their ordering us up in such a hurry. I think that the account of Wheeler's operations on the Rl. Rd. in Sherman's rear has been exaggerated or Sherman could not have sustained his army here this long. I do not know where nor what Wheeler is doing now and the Yankees may have the roads all in jimmy order by this time.

I have got me a Yankee horse but he is very poor and his back is in such a bad fix that I cannot ride him for some time to come. He was captured the day that we went out to look for the Yankees and I gave $25.00 for him. If I can get his back well and get him fat he will be worth $1,000.00 in this market.

This is a good country where we now are and is different from any of Georgia that I have seen, being level and no rocks. The land is good, but there is some poor country between this and Atlanta.

Mary, I have written you a very disconnected letter but I had to write in a bustle and by peace meals. I would have been glad to have given you a history of all that I have seen and heard for the last ten days but it would have taken a quire of paper to do so.

Mary, if you write be shure to direct your letters to the Pioneer Corps, Loring's Division, for if it be sent to Adams' Brigade or the 43d Regt. it might be some days before I get it. The Brigade Pioneer Corps are broken up and put into ranks.

Mary, in as much as I do not get many letters from you I will have to adopt the rule of writing you but once a week for it is a very hard thing for me to keep up a correspondence when the writing is all on one side. But it may be that my letters do not reach you and you are grieved as I am at not hearing from me. Laura's letter was very short and she said that you had come down to Bellefontaine and would write. Newt said the same. His was an interesting letter but said nothing of your affairs as he expected you to write. I will close this letter but I do not know how I will get it to the Post office yet.

Do not cease to pray for me.

Yours as Ever,
W. H. Berryhill

The following portion of a letter had no reference as to date. It is included in this space because of content, and because the paper he wrote it on was the same as used on the previous letter.

Everything appears to be quiett about here now. I heard a fiew guns fire up the river yesterday and day before which was said to be ours and the Yankee scouts firing upon each other, but I would as soon think that it was some Rebs shooting hogs as any thing else. It was reported yesterday that there was a 40 days truce between the United States and the Confederate States, but I reckon it is all a humbug. If such a thing should happen it would close the fighting. I do not look for much more fighting in this quarter soon.

Mary, I want you to continue to write untill I get a letter from you and tell me what you have named our new babe. I would be very glad to see it. You wrote me that it was ugly. I suppose then that you do not think that the new issue looks as well as the old, but 2 of the new issue is worth one of the old.

The letter I received from Emma stated that Bud was going to school to Mr. McDowell at the Robertson home. How do the children learn under him. How do they like him, and how for a teacher do you think he is.

How are you getting along without money. I could furnish you $100.00 now if I had any means of getting it to you. I am afraid to send it by mail for I do not know that you have got any of my letters for the last two months. George got a letter from his Henry last week which stated that Byron and James Gore were at the point of death. I learn that Dock got one from Newt that stated the same. Write me wheather they have recovered or not.

I wrote to Uncle Frank 2 weeks ago. I saw Newt, he was well. I hear no talk of any of the army going to Va. now. The farmers are making molasses here now. I get biscuits and molasses occasionally. I have never suffered for anything to eat yet, but I have studied about home until my hair has nearly all fell off.

Mary, pray for my safe return.

                      Yours as Ever,
                      W. H. Berryhill

Lovejoy Station, Ga., Friday, Sept. 9th, 1864

My Dear Niece,

    I received your nice little letter of the 26th August several days ago but have been too busy to answer it untill now. I need not tell you that Atlanta has gone up for you will have heard of it long before this letter reaches you. We left Atlanta on Thursday night the 1st of Sept. at 10 o'clock and arrived here by a circuitous route on Saturday morning about 10 o'clock. We only rested from five o'clock Friday evening untill 2 o'clock Saturday morning.

    Gen. Hardee fell back from Jonesboro to this place on Thursday. We formed line of battle on his left and on the west side of the Macon Rail Road. Hardee had been skirmishing and fighting the Yanks here for two days before we got here. They had followed him right on from where he and Lee had fought them some days before. Our army remained in line Saturday, Sunday and Monday, but on Monday night the Yankees retreated and have gone back to Atlanta, which is some 25 or 30 miles north of this. We have gone into camp and I think that the fighting is over for the present.

    The two armies are further apart now than they have been since last winter. Both armies are run down and will have to take a resting spell now. We were in line of battle almost constantly for 120 days, and we have cut ditches enough in Ga. to reach across the Confederacy.

    We lost a good deal of army supplies in Atlanta and nearly 100 cars. The cars, ammunition and c. were burned. The fire made a light so that we could see very well to travel five miles away. Gen. Johnston never lost anything on his retreats and the whole army wishes that he was our General still, for he is the best Gen. in the Confederacy.

    Tom brought me letters from you, Appalona, Laura and Newton, but none from Mary. Can you explain why it is that I am getting no letters from her for I have got none from her since the 19th July . . .

This letter dated September 18, 1864, was the most faded of all the letters, and has the most blanks because we were unable to make out words, lines, even paragraphs. The information we were able to read seemed to make enough sense to include it.

Flint River, Clayton Co., Ga., Sunday, Sept. 18, 1864

Dear Brother,

    I received a letter from you by Tom but I have passed through so many scenes of late and have written so many in last three weeks that I do not know for the life of me whether I have answered your last one or not. I think, though, I have for I always make it a point to answer every letter that I get.

    We left the command yesterday was a week ago and came down here [5 miles] to build a bridge across Flint River. We finished it last night at midnight in time and Hdqrs. is passing me and crossing the new they are going across to the side at 9 o'clock reach here which will be about Monday. Newt, you must excuse the haste with which this letter is written corps of Infantry with artiliary and any amount of wagons passing of me and almost near enough to brush my elbow

    Newt, I have received no letter from Mary in two months. I can not tell what the cause can be that her letters never reach me. She has generally mailed her letters and no one ever attemps to explain why she did not write by Tom. I got 4 or 5 letters on each of his trips from other sources but none from her and Tom can give me no satisfaction about it. He says that he brought all the letters that was gave to him and that's all that he knows about it. I should think nothing strange in not getting a letter from Mary if no one else were getting letters from Choctaw. Everybody else are getting letters from there and I get them occasionally from other sources. I can not see why her's do not get through as well as others. People in Mississippi write regularly.

    I am well　　　　　the boys generally were well when I left them yesterday a week ago. George started to the hospital the day that Tom got here but did not stop there but a fiew days. He came back the day that I left the command to go in　　　　so bad at the hospital that he would not stay　　　from him yesterday evening. He was not well　　　up and about. Newt, I have no news to write　　Yankees appear to be resting at Atlanta.
    will reinforce Grant

Your brother,
W. H. Berryhill

Chattahoochee River, Campbell Co., Ga.,
Friday, Sept. 28, 1864

My Dear Son,

    It has been some time since I have written to you and a longer time since I have got a letter from you, so I have concluded to write you a short letter to let you know that I am still in the land of the living and how and where I am. We are now fortifying on the Chattahoochee River five miles below Campbelltown. Our line extends from the river in an east course to the West Point Rail Road and I do not know how much farther. We are South of West Point and Atlanta and 25 miles from it. I am told that there are no Yanks nearer than Sandtown, which is 12 miles above this on the Chattahoochee. I do not know anything of Gen. Hood's plans and I do not know either wheather there is any prospect of another fight soon or not. I have heard no booming of cannons now for nearly three weeks, a thing that has not happened before since I have been in the State of Ga. I am in tolerable good health but I had a bad pain in my back and head some days ago, but it is nearly well now.

Bud, I am out in the woods sitting on a log where my corps is at work, writing you this letter. Do you think that you would write me a letter if you had to set on an old knot log to write. The weather has been showery for the last five or six days and is still cloudy and a prospect of more rain. I will be glad when it clears up.

We built a bridge across Flint River in Clayton Co. last week. I wrote several letters while there. I hope that you have got them. We left there last Sunday evening and camped near Fayetteville that night and the next day we went to Palometto on the West Point Rail Road where I sent a letter to your Uncle Newton. The next day [Tuesday] we came to the river. Adams' Brigade is some 3 or 4 miles from here between this and the Rl. Rd. I was at Co. D a little while day before yesterday. George was tolerable well. The Captain and the boys generally were well.

I have got a fine repeating rifle. It shoots seven times with one loading. I went into a little corn patch to pull some crab grass for my horse and a negro picked up the gun in the fence corner where I suppose some Yankee had left it. I gave the negro $17 for it. I suppose it is worth some $200. If I could manage to get it home I would make you a present of it, but the chance is bad to ever get it there.

When Tom came he brought me letters from Newton, Laura, Emma and Appalona. I answered all of them. It has now been near a month since these letters were written and I have received no letter since from any one. The last letter that I got from your Ma was written more than 2 months ago. I reckon that I will get a basketfull of letters some of these days. George got a letter from Henry last week which said that Byron and Jimmy were at the point of death. I would like to hear from them. Write soon to your Pa.

W. H. Berryhill

Sweetwater River or Creek, Cobb Co., Ga.
Saturday, Oct. 1st, 1864

My Dear Wife,
    I received your letter of the 28th Aug. some three days ago. I have had no chance to get a letter off since, as we have been on the move since I received your letter. It was just a month on the road. It was to have been sent by J. M. Norwood, but it was post marked at Columbus, Miss. I do not know when I will get this off and only have time to write a very short letter now.
    We crossed the Chattahoochee River last Thursday the 29th Sept. and took a north course untill we came to this big creek which is about the size of Big Black at Greensboro. We were engaged yesterday for half the day in repairing a bridge that the Yanks had torn up and have been resting since. The army is some 2-1/2 miles behind us, except one brigade which is here at the bridge on picket.
    Jackson's and Armstrong's Caverly have gone to the front up about Lost Mountain. We are about 17 miles from where we crossed the Chattahoochee River and 15 miles from Marietta and 12 miles from New Hope Church where the first battle was fought in Cobb Co. and on the 24th of last May. We have flanked Atlanta. We are North west of it and some 25 or 30 miles from it. I do not know wheather the whole army is along or not. All that I know is that Stewart's Corps is here and it is said that Lee's and Hardee's are along. We came ahead of the Infantry all the way. I do not know what will be the next move. We may go towards Blue Mountain, Ala., or we may go to the rail road about Marietta. It is a bold move and may do a great deal if the army can subsist up here, but I have some fears of that as we are so far from the rail road.

Mary, we are fixing to move our camp back to headQ. which is 2 miles from here. If I have a chance I will write more. I am well. I have written this in a great hurry. Excuse errors. I have only got this one letter of the 28th Aug. from you since the 18th July. Do not be discouraged because your letters do not reach me, but write again.

Your Billy

Brownsville Post Office, Ga.,
Saturday Evening, Oct. 1st, 1864

My Dear Sons,

    I wrote your dear Ma a short letter this morning but I had to write in such a hurry that I do not know that she can make sense of it or not. So I will try to write you a fiew lines and send with it. But it keeps raining so that I cannot write to do much good. I am sitting in a wagon trying to keep my paper dry while I write. I am now at a little cross roads Post Office called Brownsville in Paulding Co., Ga. I camped on Sweetwater River last night in Cobb Co. but we left there today at 1 o'clock and came back the road we traveled yesterday 3 miles to where Loring's Division is in camp. I do not know how long we will stay here, but I think not many days, nor I do not know where we will go next.

    There is no Yanks near us, I suppose not nearer than Rail Road at Marietta which is some 18 miles from where I now am. Our caverly has gone out about day. Some caverly tore up some of the Rl. Rd. above Marietta a fiew days ago and burned three trains of cars and captured a drove of beef cattle from a Yankee slaughter pen. I saw the cattle today. They were mostly large oxen. They were said to be Illinois cattle.

I seldom ever hear from home now and most of what I do hear is from letters that others receive. And now that we have left the Rail Roads I reckon that I never will hear from home again, but do not stop writing for we will be apt to get to some Rl. Rd. that will bring letters to us. If we go to Blue Mountain, Ala. our letters will reach us sooner than they did at Atlanta.

Well, boys, are you good, kind and obedient children. I hope you are and do not give your Ma any extra trouble with you. Now I want you to be good boys all the time so that your Ma can give a good account of your conduct when I come home to see you all, and so every one of you can come right up to me and say, "Pa, I have been a good boy all this long time that you have been gone." Then you see I will be very proud of you. My girls must be good, too. Laura used to be a good girl, but how is Mattie, Lizzie, and, and, and, what is her name. Well, that is bad. Got a little girl and do not know her name. But maybe her name is Mary for your Ma said in that big letter that she and your Uncle Ira sent me in August that she reckoned she would call her Mary "partly." Then it will be Tonia, Mattie, Lizzie and Mollie.

You must not think strange of my writing on these old receipts, orders, and blanks and c. I picked up a handful of them as we came out from Atlanta and as one side of them is blank it will do to write upon and save the expense of buying paper, which is very high at this time.

I will send this letter by Mr. Turner of the Pioneer Corps who is to start to Miss. in the morning. He will mail at Mayhew. I do not know when I will get to come home, but I shall try very hard to get to come to see you this winter. Kiss your Ma for me.

                    Your Affectionate Father,
                    W. H. Berryhill

P.S. Tell your Ma that I did not have the chance to look over her letter while I was writing and therefore I did not answer it, but will do it in my next if there is anything that needs attention. I recollect one item that was in it which was that she had heard that thread was selling at $25. in Ga. I have never seen a bale since I have been in the State. I do not know what they are selling thread at in Ga., but everything else is higher here than any place that I have ever been.

Pa

Alabama

Two Miles West of Gailsville, Cherokee Co., Ala.
Tuesday, Oct. 18th 1864

My Dear Wife,
 I closed a letter to you night before last intending to send it out by the Brigade mail, but I missed it not withstanding I got up two hours before day. I afterwards saw a quartermaster going to Blue Mountain and I gave it to him to be mailed there. I have written you three letters since we started on the Rd. The first one at Brownsville Post Office I sent out by a man going to Miss. to be mailed at Mayhew, Miss. The second one I gave to a man at Cedartown, Polk Co., Ga., who said that he would carry it to where it could be mailed, and the 3d, as I stated above. These three letters gave an account of all our travels and marches and doings since we crossed the Chattahoochee River. I hope you have got them. I have received   that you wrote soon after the birth of little Mary. I received one of them since we have been on this raid. It was dated the 19th Sept. and is the one that had little Lizzie's greasy fingerprints on it. I wish I could see the little soul. Tell Miss Mattie that I would like to see her, too. Then there is little Mary. As a matter of course I would like to see her. But I would not know her if I were to meet her in the road, for you see that I have so many children that I do not know them all. You say that she is ugly. I reckon it is quite enough to have one ugly one in the family, for all the rest are beauties. Little Mary must be well educated to pass her through the world.
 Yesterday morning, Monday the 17th, the troops were put in motion two hours before day. Our place on a march is in front of the Division, but yesterday morning we got no orders. So we did not leave camp untill daylight. The Gen. thought of us when he found that we were not in front and sent a currier back for us. We did not go more than 4 miles before the column was halted and we lay around for some six hours, then went into camp untill this morning five o'clock.

We camped night before last one mile from Summerville and last night five miles from it. Summerville is the county cite of Chatooga Co., Ga., and is a little better than Greensboro in appearance, with two or three very pretty churches. Gailsville is on the bank of Chattooga River and is about Greensboro's equal in appearance. We have marched some 18 miles today right down the Chattooga Valley. We crossed the river one mile before we reached Summerville and have come down the stream all the way. I do not suppose that we were more than 8 miles from it at any time. We had a splendid road to day and through a rich country. The road from Summerville to this place runs in a south west direction. I would like verry well to live in this country in times of peace but the Yankees have raided through this country and have damaged the people a great deal.

Since we left Dalton we have been going in the direction of Blue Mountain which is our base at this time, but I have no idea where we will go to before we are done. If you will notice in my other letters I have ventured several times to say where we were going but have missed so often that I have quit saying what I think.

We are 25 miles west of Rome, 14 from Cave Springs, some 50 from Blue Mountain and about 50 to the Tennessee River. Hood keeps his own secrets and there is not a General in this army knows what he is going to do. I think that he has Sherman worse puzzeled than he has ever been before. I do not know where Sherman's army is. We never hear anything here. It has been reported several times that Sherman had left Atlanta. I do not know wheather it is so or not. I can not see how he can stay there with the Rail Road destroyed. I know that that is done for I have seen it myself. Some 20 miles of it destroyed above Resaca and 12 or 14 below the Ettawa river.

I have not been well for the last two days. I have a severe cold and it has settled in my back and I am sore all

over, but am very well able to ride. George was quite sick yesterday morning and I got him off on the supply train to 15th command. Dock
Jimmy is well. I saw him this morning. He was in command of the slow train as we call it, which is the barefooted, sore footed and those that are sick but not sick enough to be sent to the hospital. They are not required to march in ranks but to get along the best they can. Truss Smith, George Monts, Capps and McCain were sent to Blue Mountain on the sick list 2 days ago. The troops are in good spirits, but are badly broken down in having marched more than 200 miles in the past 20 days. It is camp talk that we will rest here tomorrow. Perhaps I will write more before I have a chance to send this letter off.

> Yours as ever,
> W. H. Berryhill

Gadsden, Ala., Thursday, Oct. 20th, 1864

Dear Mary,

I stop for a fiew minutes at this place to finish and mail this letter as there is a post office here. Gadsden is on the Coosa river 28 miles from Blue Mountain. Yesterday, 19th, we continued down the Chattooga river for a fiew miles and crossed Little river and kept down the Coosa Valley with Lookout Mountain on our right. We started at 8 o'clock yesterday morning and marched 15 miles. We started at 3 this morning and have already made 14 miles at 10 a.m. We thought that we were going to Jacksonville, but we have turned north again taking the Gunters Landing road. Gunters Landing is on the Tennessee River 45 miles from here.

I got a letter from Ira by Marshall Rose last night dated 10th inst. A little post script at the top said that you and Mattie had just arrived at his house and all were well. He also said that you were going to move to Bellefontaine. You can just do as you think best.

I am well pleased with the results of the election. Ira got more votes than anyone else in the County. Old Plut [?] is badly beaten. I also got a letter from Newton Berryhill by mail of the same date. He said you were talking of moving to his place and had left there the day before. I can not answer their letters now. Newt's also stated that you had written by Lieut. McLarty. He has not arrived yet that I know of. It looks like your letters never get through. I expected a letter by Rose from you but he says he did not see you.

I think at this time that we will go up about Huntsville and Decatur and perhaps in to Tenn. I am better of my cold but have had diarhea to day and last night. Do not be discouraged but write again. Pray for me that I may come through safe. May God Bless you. Ever yours.

W. H. Berryhill

Near Cortland, Ala., Saturday Evening, Oct. 29th, 1864
My Dear Wife,

I am determined to write you by every opportunity and to do that I must keep a letter always on hand ready to send off by any opportunity that offers its self. I sent out a letter day before yesterday by Col. Sykes who went to Columbus, Miss. to carry the body of his Brother [Adj. Sykes] who was killed in front of Decatur. There was no further attempt made on Decatur than was made the first evening that we got there. The Yankees reinforced from the time that we got there untill we left. I have no doubt but what we could have taken the place but it was so well fortified that it would have cost the lives of more men than the place could have been worth to us. And Gen. Hood issued an order to the troops when we started on this raid saying that he would not force them to charge any strongly fortified positions and he has only carried out his word. But the troops would have pitched into this place very willingly from all that I could see or hear.

There was nothing done yesterday [Friday 28th] but sharpshooting and shelling each other and running batteries up at different points on the river to shell the Gunboats. They moved their position every time our guns were brought to bear upon them. The Yanks charged and captured one of our batteries but the 21st Miss. Regt. came up just at the time and made them fly from there in a hurry. The half of them were negroes. Jo Golding got one of his arms cut off by a shell yesterday. It was cut with such force that it [his hand] fell 30 yds. from him.

We left there at sun rise this morning. Soon after I started I came up with Capt. Gilbert sick and scarcely able to travel. I gave him my horse and took it afoot. I walked 12 miles at quick time [!] without resting once. He then got into Stephen Bennett's wagon and I made the balance of the way. We have come about 20 miles to day. I do not know where we will strike next.

Clayton, Ala., Sunday, Oct. 30th. We continued our march down the rail road to day. We got into Courtland at sunrise. It has been a very pretty little place before the war but now like all other Southern towns it is going reck. We marched about 15 miles to day and camped at Clayton or Leyton, I do not know which. It is a small place, a station on the Rl. Rd. 10 miles East from Tuscumbia.

I saw Capt. Gilbert in a wagon at Courtland early this morning. He looked very bad. He went on to Tuscumbia and I don't know where from there for I do not know where our hospital will be established. I gave him a couple of buiskets for he had nothing but some cold corn bread. He may get   from the hospital   come to Choctaw. He can tell you all about my position and how I am getting along.

    The Troops are suffering now for something to eat for this country has nothing in it to feed an army. They have been living on bread for several days. My Mess has plenty of flour. We bought 150 lbs. the day before we got out of Ga.

    I saw Gen. Beauregard this morning for the first time, though he has been with us a good part of our trips. He is a keen looking Frenchman. His head and mustache is white. He is in command of this department. The Troops have great confidence in him. Hood still commands the Army of Tenn.

    Mary, Latham did not come. I have not seen McLarty but he sent me word that Latham turned back and Capt. Thornton is to come with him and he left my socks at Thornton's to bring on when he comes. As usual, I reckon I shall never get them. There are many soldiers here that are barefooted but some of them are being shod occasionally.

    I will write more tomorrow.

                        Billy

We surrounded Decatur on Wednesday the 26th Oct. and I thought we were going to storm it as the enemies force was said to be small, but after laying close to their works for 3 days we raised the siege and came to this place--45 miles. We left Decatur Saturday morning and arrived here Monday morning, 9 o'clock, and have been resting since.

    The Yankees shelled us severely at Decatur. The 43d lost about 12 killed and wounded, three. Killed among them was Adj. Sykes, the best man in the Regt. He asked before he died if he had made an enemy in the Regt. If so he wished to see them to know the cause. But I have no idea that one could be found. His place cannot be filled as it was before and he will never be forgotten as long as the name of the 43d lasts.

The Yankees remained as long as we stayed at Decatur and the place was too well fortified and not considered of sufficient importance to sacrifice many men for. I do not know that the intention was to attempt to take this place, but only to make a front there to draw the forces to that point while Lee moved his corps on Florence, which he took on Sunday and affected a crossing there. The most of Lee's Corps has been across the Tennessee River but the whole army is on this side now, but pontoons are tyed below Florence ready to cross at any time. But the troops were in
. . . .

Tuscumbia, Ala., Monday, Oct. 31st, 1864

My Dear Wife,

We left Leyton this morning at daybreak and arrived at Tuscumbia before 9 o'clock A.M. We have gone into camps here but I do not know how long we will remain here, but I suppose long enough to get us supplies of shoes, clothing and rations and c. I learn that Lee's Corps has captured Florence and has crossed the Tenn. River. Florence is five miles from here. Lee shelled the Yanks out before crossing. He captured a fiew prisoners. Stewart's Corps is all camped here. I do not know where Cheatham [Hardee] is, but all three corps keep in striking distance of each other. I think the intention is for the whole army to cross the Tennessee River and perhaps strike for Nashville. If it does not do that I have no idea what it will do, unless we make a raid on Memphis.

I rode around and took a look at Tuscumbia. It has been a right fast place before this war, but it looks desolate now. A portion of it has been burned, I suppose by Yankee hands.

Mary, I have frequently written to you of passing through the prettiest country that I ever saw, but I say now that the Tennessee Valley is the prettiest country in the world. It is one continuous farm for 50 miles or more where we struck it above Decatur. This country is level and you can have an open view as far as your eyes will let you see. But there is but very little of it in cultivation now. The Yankees have destroyed every thing but the Negro cabins and I do not recollect seeing a dwelling house left standing on the road from Courtland to this place, except that little town we camped at last night [25 miles]. All have been burned, but the Negro houses are still there, but I could see a good many fine buildings a good way off from the road.

If we stop here I hope to get letters from you, as the mails are in operation to this place. Direct your letters to Tuscumbia for I think that it will be our base of operations for the present. The Rail Road is in operation to within some 12 or 14 miles from Iuka and some 45 miles from Corinth, about due east. I am about 150 or 160 miles of home now. I am nearer home now that I have been since I left Demopolis, and if I had a furlough I would ride home in about three days with what I would borrow of the nights, but I see no prospect of a thing of that sort now. How I would like to pay you all a visit now and tell you of the many things that I have seen and heard, and to hear your sweet voices once more, and then the merry shouts and happy laughs of the children.

I got a letter from you last week, dated Aug. 21st. You speak of Laura's profession of religion in this letter. I had heard of it long since by letters from others. You say that you advised her to wait a while before joining a church and become well acquainted with the rules, faith, regulations, and usuages of the different churches before joining. "Procrastination is the thief of time," and I should not have thrown anything in the way of her joining any church that she desired. I should not insist upon her very strenously to unite with the church, but I should advise her to do so as the best protection against the snares of the wicked one. I would rather that she was in the church that I belong to, but I do not insist upon it if she prefers any other. I ought to have written to her on the subject long since, but I am not still long enough at a place to write a letter on the subject of religion. You and Laura must not forget to pray for me. Kiss the babies for me.

       Yours Affectionately,
       W. H. Berryhill

Cherokee Station, Ala., Saturday, November 5th, 1864

My Dear Wife,

    I drop you a fiew lines today merely to let you know that I am in the land of the living and am well. This station is 16 miles from Tuscumbia and is as far as the cars are running, but the road will be repaired to the next station above this in a fiew days which is 4 miles further up.

    The army has been resting at Tuscumbia since last Monday where they are getting shoes, clothing, rations and c., all of which they have been suffering for very badly. I think they will be well supplied in a day or so more and then I think they will set out to cross the Tennessee River. Lee's Corps are already across and are fortified on the north side.

    I have not been with the army since Thursday evening. We have been repairing the dirt road to this place. We found the road cut up badly but there are hundreds of wagons passing over it daily.

    Mary, I have but a moment to write you for I will have to start back to Tuscumbia directly. I have no news to write you. I have written to you, Newt and Ira since I got to Tuscumbia. I hope you will all get the letters.

    Mary, I sent up an application for a 30 days leave of absence this morning. I have but little idea that it will be approved but if I do not begin the make an effort and keep making them I will never get off. I will hate to come home without money, but I want to see you so bad I will come if I get a chance if I have to beg my way home. If I should happen to succeed in getting off I will be at home in 10 or 12 days, but you need not look for me for I have but little faith in getting off. Write to me soon.

                          Yours as ever
                          W. H. Berryhill

South Florence, Ala., Sunday Evening, Nov. 13th, 1864

Dear Ira,

 I received your letter of the 26 Oct. to day and I received one about a week ago dated the 13th. I will try to answer them but will have to be short.

 I am sorrow to hear of Ada's continued bad health. Your fate is like mine. We both live with a sickly wife. Some men become impatient, disgusted, and tired out with a wife that is frequently sick. But it always made mine feel double dear to me and I always felt that I was not as kind to her as I ought to be and do the best I could. I always found that she could do more and show more kindness to me when I was sick than I ever did for her. A man can never be too kind to a sick wife. I hope you will never grow tired waiting on your wife, let her illness be long or short. A man never even begins to appreciate the love, kindness and affections of a wife until he gets sick in the army away from home and away from friends. There was a time in the history of this war when a sick soldier was cared for and assisted by all that saw him, but now he is shunned by nearly every one as they would a pestilence. I have had the good fortune to escape sickness since leaving Mississippi last spring. I do not think that I have been excused from duty for a single day on account of sickness since I have been with the Army of Tennessee.

 I have been at this place [South Florence] nearly a week. Stewart's Corps is still near Tuscumbia, which is five miles from here. It was expected to move here where I am here with the Pioneer Corps, but on account of the sudden rise in the river the pontoons could not be kept in crossing order. In fact, all crossing was suspended for some 4 days and was only got in crossing order late yesterday evening.

 Lee's Corps has been over some 10 or 12 days. Cheatham's Corps crossed this morning. He got his infantry and part of his train over safe, but had a large drove of beef cattle to cross. After getting a portion of them over some large and rather wild steers got into a stampede and made such a rush for the opposite shore that they crowded off every thing on before them, falling off into the boats sinking several of them and causing the bridge to break. Some 80 head of cattle went down the river. They swam from a half to a mile and a half. I think they have about all been saved. Several men were knocked over too, but do not think there was any loss of life. One man went down with his horse which swam with him for more than a mile down the river before he could make a landing.

Cheatham's artiliary and a train of wagons some 2 miles in length is still on this side of the bridge. One broke about 12 to day and it will be after dark before it will be ready for crossing again. Stewart's Corps was ordered to start here at today but they have not arrived. I presume their orders has been countermanded on account of the break in the bridge. Cheatham will not get fully out of the way before 10 o'clock tomorrow. The impression I get is that will not go to Tennessee but will remain here to hold this from coming out some down on this side and cutting off our supplies from Corinth.

I was at the 43d today Bob Cook. The boys generally were well. George, Dock, Truss and others have gone to the hospital some time ago. We have had a great deal of rain for the last three weeks 3 or 4 days it has been clear and cold. We have been camped in an old store where there is a number of bales of cotton and a bale cut open and opened out makes a good bed, so we sleep as snug as bugs.

You speak of occupying my Greensboro place next year. Any arrangement you make with Mary is all right with me. I have no idea when I will ever get home again. I made application for a 30 days leave of absence last week but it was disapproved. Mary is much in need of money now and I can do nothing for her. There is $675 pay due me but I can not tell when I will get it. The government is acting very badly in not paying the troops. I am very much distressed on account of the destitute condition of my family, but can do nothing for them. But I trust in God and feel that he will not let them suffer more than they can bear.

It is getting too dark to write so Good Bye, My Brother.
W. H. Berryhill

An indication of the "destitute condition" of families in Greensboro, Choctaw County, Mississippi, is revealed in this article from the Greensboro *Southern Motive* which was published a few months before this, on May 7, 1864 —

Ma, I Want a Piece of Bread

THERE IS SCARCELY a day passes but what we see three or four ladies come to town for the purpose of getting from the Commissioner, a little meal and meat with which to feed their almost starved children. But owing to the impossibility of the commissioners procuring meat, these poor women are compelled to go home without it, and frequently, we are told, without any corn or meal. Thus the poor women—the families of soldiers—are tormented by the agonizing cry of their children by calling for—"Ma, I want a piece of bread." Think of that mother's feelings when she has not nor knows not where to get the bread. The commissioners have tried in vain to buy meat but they cannot for neither love nor money because it is not to be had in the county. We wrote on this subject before, appealing to the Government authorities to sell the corn and meat that would be collected in this county, to the families here that were actually in want, knowing at the same time there would be great scarcity in provisions in this county, and for them to purchase where these commodities were plentiful. We are informed that there is an abundance of corn in the prairies close by the railroad. It is well known to every one who has resided in this county any length of time, that before the war broke out, the people would have to send to the prairies for corn and buy their meat from the market. This was when her working population was at home. This is a poor county, and two-thirds her working class of people are in the army, and their families left, helpless on the remaining portion for support. It is expected by the Government, it appears, that these families are to support their brothers, their sons and their husbands, who are in the army, when it took all they could make to support their families when they were at home. There are but very few negroes in the county, and the people will suffer if something is not done to prevent it— Already have some of the destitute families felt the effects of the approaching crisis. Corn can scarcely be bought at any price—and as for meat we do not know of a pound for sale. How can we then expect long to have an army of true veterans in the field and their wives and little ones at home without anything to eat. We can remedy this evil and let us come up boldly to their relief.

Tennessee

Near Columbia, Tenn., Monday, Nov. 28th, 1864

My Dear Wife,

    I write this letter to you but do not know when I will get to send it out for I know of no mail communication from Tenn. to Miss. We crossed the Tennessee line on Saturday the 19th. It was raining a very cold rain and we were on the bridge for an hour and a half or more on account of wagons stalling on the Island ahead.

    After crossing the river we passed through Florence which is a very nice town not quite as large as Columbus, Miss. We took a road leading N. E. to Shale Creek, 9 miles from Florence. Our pickets were on one side and the Yankees on the other. We were to make a bridge on Shale Creek but the Yanks were firing across the stream so we could not work that evening, and the night was so dark that we could not see to work so we put off the work untill next morning.

    Gen. Brantley was on picket up there with his brigade. I went to see him on business Saturday evening, Saturday night and Sunday morning. I have never been treated with more politeness and kindness by any officer since I have been in the service. I can not see that promotion has given him the "big head" in the least for he is the same Old Bill Brantley yet. Sweatman and Frank Holloway are on his staff. Frank always appears to be as glad to see me as he would be to see a brother.

    Sunday the 20th Still cold. We worked on the bridge untill 2 o'clock when orders came to stop the work and return to the Division which would camp at the fork of the road 2 miles back where it would turn to the left in nearly a due north direction. Our wagon was gone after rations so we remained at our Saturday night's camp.

    Monday the 21st was cold. We set out at day light and found our Div. 2 miles back on the road we had come. They were still in camp and did not move untill 10 o'clock. The pioneers were ordered right ahead but I took time to go by my Regt. When I got to it I found that B. F. McCain had got in and brought me 2 letters, one from Newt and one from you that you had started by George who had stopped at Embry's sick, so I was informed by McCain. I was truly sorrow to hear that you were all in bad health and especially John's continued bad health. Poor little fellow. I fear he will always have bad health. Be careful with him and do not let him get any knocks on his head. I have never heard wheather Willie has ever got over that rupture or not.

You say that you can get $600 for my Greensboro lot and ask if you must sell. I am somewhat astonished at you for asking the question for I have told you repeatedly to do with every thing as you thought best, and you know that I wished to sell the place and would have sold it last winter for $500 if you had not been opposed to my selling it, for you said that you wished to reserve a home for you and our children in case I should never get back. If you sell for $600 you get $100 more than I gave for it. And you need the money.

If I could have been at the Brigade the day that I crossed the river I could have drawn $180, but it would not have been of any benefit to you for I had no means of sending it to you. I will try to get my horse to you by spring if I do not lose him. I have got him a little crippled. The day that we crossed the river it was raining and the road was full of water and he fell suddenly into a hole up to his shoulders, and in scrambling to get out he cut his left fore leg on the inside of the knee joint and he has been lame since. He is a little stiff, too, but if I had him at home where he could be rested a little I would not take a $1000 for him.

About the time I left my regt. on Monday it set into snowing and continued by storms till late in the evening when the sun would show itself occasionally. The wind was high and we had a bitter cold time of it, but I had on 2 prs.

drawers and three shirts. One pr. of the drawers and one shirt was wollen, but I had lost my gloves and my hands suffered. I had one good sock, too, that I got in the Yankee quarters, The Ackworth. I put it on one foot over the old ragged one, and the other foot I robed up with a wool rag. The legs of the socks were all good.

We camped at a mill where there was lots of planks. We made good shelters to break off the wind, made large fires and slept well.

Tuesday 22d. Everything was frozen as hard as a brick and I saw icickles [or logs of ice as you always please to call them] six feet long and 3 or 4 inches thick at the large end. We stayed at our camp untill 2 o'clock waiting for the Div. to come up and when it came up I saw Capt. Thornton and Henry Latham in the ranks. The Captain had a letter for me from you. Not as late a date as the one by McCain but I read it with as much interest as the other. Latham still had those socks that you had started to me more than a month before. They came in a good time and I reckon that I appreciate them more highly than I would have done if I had got them in warmer weather.

We marched this day untill after dark. We crossed the Tennessee line into Wayne Co. about sunset. We had snow in the fore part of the day. It fell very fast at times and from every little cloud that passed over. At times it would be falling fast while the sun was shining.

Wednesday, 23d. Continued the march at sun rise in a N.E. direction. The ground was frozen harder than the day before but the wind not so high and it was not so cold traveling and about mid day it thawed a little on top, but froze again at night. We camped this night on the banks of a beautiful running creek near the house of Old Man Hollis, the father of a celebrated Tory or bush whacking Captain. The old man was put under arrest and carried on the next day, but being an old man he was let return to his home the next night. His property was badly used up by the troops and I think that it would all have been destroyed if gards had not been put over it.

The people all through Wayne and part of Laurence are three forths of them Union Tories and it is dangerous for single individuals and small parties to pass through their neighborhoods. But not withstanding the murderous disposition of the men, I must say that I think that their families were badly treated in many instances by our troops, and not only the Tory families but frequently the families of Confederates, for nearly everything is destroyed where this army goes.

Thursday, 24th.

We marched up the creek valley that we had camped on. There was a high hill on each side of the narrow valley and the creek ran first to one side and then to the other so that we had to cross it 18 times in going 5 or 6 times [he obviously meant miles]. These creek valleys are very rich and the people live well. They have lots of cows and fat hogs, and are living as if the war was not going on. The road that we had been traveling for the last 4 days was verry narrow but at night we struck a large turnpike road leading from Waynesboro to Columbia. This was a verry pleasant day for walking except the sloppy road in the after part of the day, for this hard frozen ground has all turned to mud and water.

Friday, 25th.

Marched at sun rise on the pike road leading to Columbia. We marched about 15 hours and camped about 2 miles north of Henryville, Laurence Co. It rained a little during the night. Forrest had whipped the Yanks out of Henryville 2 days before and captured 2 or 3 doz. of them.

Saturday, 26th.

Set out at sunrise and got in to Murry Co. about 10

o'clock. It is a very rich county and beautiful lands and large farms. We passed through Mount Pleasant late in the evening. It is a nice town and is 10 miles south of Columbia. It is as large or larger than Tuscumbia. We camped 8 miles south of Columbia on the farm of Mr. Polk, brother to our late Gen. Polk. There was no end to the riches of the people about here before the war. The Yanks have cultivated many of the farms here this year and in many places the crop is still in the field.   through the day and a good part of the night.

Sunday, 27th.

Warm and cloudy. We set out for Columbia at sun rise. There was plenty of Yanks there and Forrest was holding them at bay and fighting them a little. We went up the pike a few miles and then turned to the right and traveled some 2 miles of the worst road I ever saw and came in to an other pike road which we traveled some 1½ miles and took to the right again over an other bad road when we struck an other large pike road which we took and traveled a half mile and struck camp some 2½ miles from Columbia. I went up on a hill in front where I could see the Yankee works and lots of Yanks. I could also see a small portion of the City. Busy preparations were being made by all hands for the fight on the morrow.

I worked untill after midnight putting in batteries. But this morning when we got up the Yanks were gone, but Forrest crossed Duck River yesterday and is after them now. I hear the cannons booming every fiew seconds. The Yankee force was estimated at 15,000 but it is said that their supplies were short. I have not been in town. There are guards to keep the troops out. If I had been in there I might have bought you some Calico and cotton cards but I reckon it is too late now.

I expect to have to move in a fiew minutes for I see them striking tents at HdQs now. I will write more when I have time but I do not know how I will ever get it to you, but I will have it ready and send it by first chance, so you may get it without its being finished. I have written on the wrong sides of this paper first but have paged it so that you can read it all right.

Monday evening, 28th.

We set out soon after writing the above and moved to the right to cross the river above town for the Yanks still hold the banks opposite the town. But the Bridge was not finished so we returned to our same camp. I have seen lots of cotton cards, calico and apron checks, but I got nothing for I was not permitted to visit the Sutlers Stores.

Near Franklin, Tenn., Thursday, Dec. 1st, 1864

Oh My Dear Wife,

We have passed through terrible scenes and death struggles since I stopped writing this letter on Monday evening, but that you may understand it all I will give an account of our marches and c. from Monday evening up to now.

Tuesday the 29th.

We set out after sunrise and crossed the river some 3½ miles above Columbia. The enemy were in full retreat but their rear gard still held the opposite of the river at the City. We moved by a circuitous route to try to get in their rear. After marching hard all day we came upon the Yanks at Spring Hill, which is some 10 miles from Columbia on the pike road. But we had marched 16 or 18 miles to get there. Forrest had been fighting them for a good while when we came up at dark, but the enemy still held the road and town and it was too dark for us to see to do any thing, so after marching around untill near 11 o'clock to get in to position we lay down to rest untill morning. Albert Spencer who is with Forrest's caverly got wounded in the head during the

THE BATTLE OF FRANKLIN, TENNESSEE

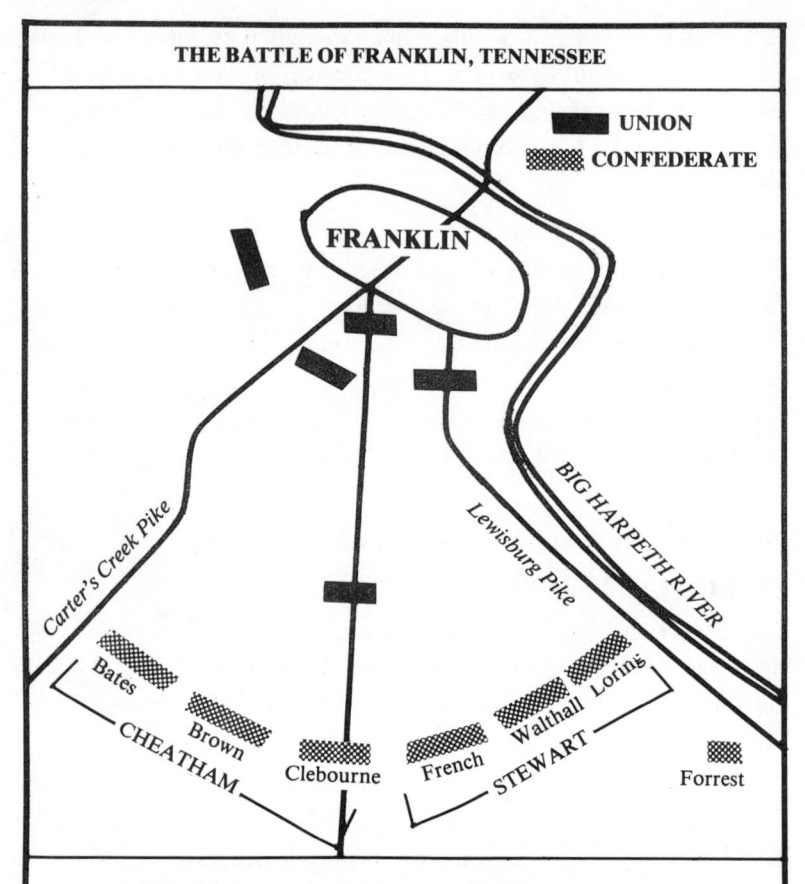

(Map showing Union and Confederate positions around Franklin, Tennessee, with the Big Harpeth River, Carter's Creek Pike, and Lewisburg Pike. Confederate forces shown: Cheatham's Corps with Bates, Brown, and Cleburne; Stewart's Corps with French, Walthall, and Loring; and Forrest.)

Co. D, 43rd Regiment, Adams' Brigade, Loring's Division, Stewart's Corps, Hood's Army of Tennessee, had, according to W. H. Berryhill's letters, suffered very few casualties until the disastrous Battle of Franklin.

Billy Berryhill was still with the Pioneer Corps and not in the line of battle during this engagement, but many of his close friends and fellow officers from Choctaw County, Mississippi, were killed here on November 30, 1864.

"Our loss there in killed and wounded will not fall short of 4,000. I think the Yankee loss is at least 1,000 less than ours." This was W. H. Berryhill's estimate of the loss at Franklin. Actually, Confederate casualties, in wounded and killed in action, were approximately 6,252, while the Union losses were about one-third this number, or 2,326.[1]

[1]Shelby Foote, *The Civil War, A Narrative—1864* (New York: Random House, 1974) pp. 668, 672, 673.

October—December, 1864   *THE GENTLE REBEL*

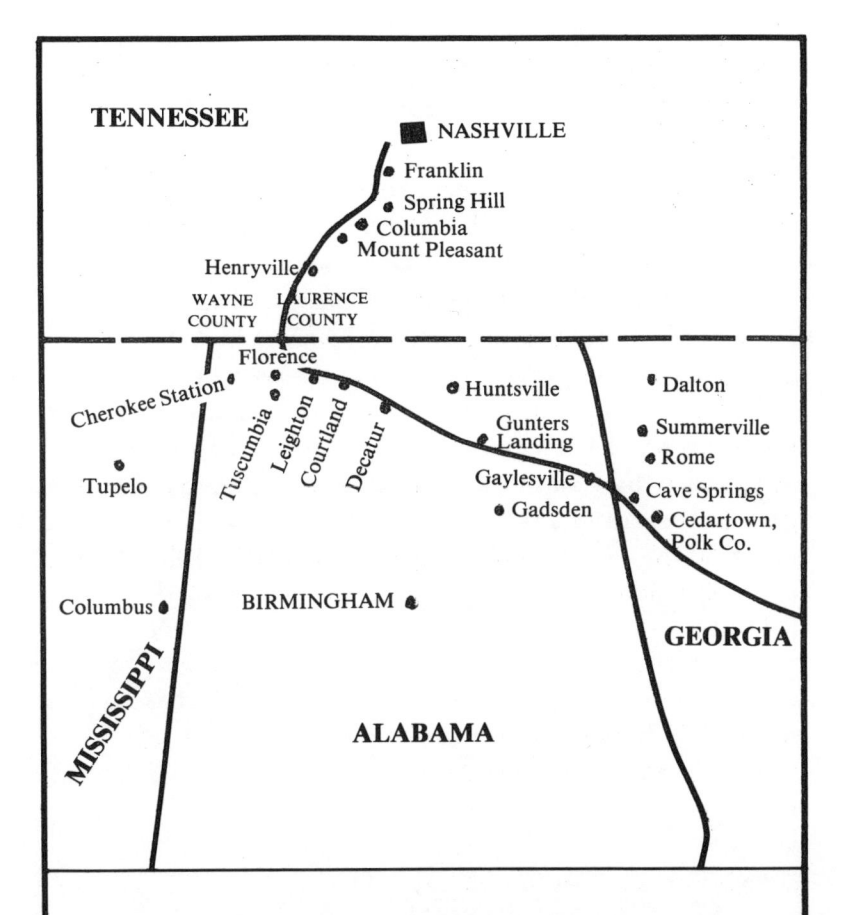

The towns and cities shown on this map are nearly all mentioned in the letters, although the line of march might not have gone through each place. Some cities, Birmingham, Columbus, and Tupelo, for instance, are shown only to put the map in proper perspective.

Billy Berryhill was killed in the Battle of Nashville, December 15, 1864, and was at that time acting Captain of Co. D. It is said that Stewart had only about 4800 men on Montgomery Hill when Gen. Thomas sent his 48,000 men to carry out his grand left wheel.[1]

This map is provided to facilitate following the progress of W. H. Berryhill and Co. D as detailed in the letters.

[1] Shelby Foote, *op. cit.*, p. 692.

day. Poor Jimmy went to see him in the night and sayed when he returned that he thought that Albert would get well.

Monday the 30th.

When day came we found that the Yanks had all gone so we set out at sun rise in pursuit. We struck the road just above Spring Hill and found that they had gone in a hurry. The road was strewn with tents, knapsacks, dirty clothing, books, papers, co. and regt. record blanks and c., and a great many wagons that they had cut the teams out and set the wagons on fire. I saw some wagons where they had killed the teams and left them. The women along the road appeared to be glad to see us and came to their gates and gave us bread and cheered us on. After some six miles march we began to come up with the Yanks and they formed a line of battle on some big hills in our front with an open field with stone fences between us and them. We threw

skirmishes and then in   by the right flank. [This was over 2 miles from Franklin, Tenn.] through Yanks   and then filed to the   The Yanks had formed a   with

skirmishing was kept up all day. The   2 miles or more   back to their works around
with 10 of the pioneers were   a battery to lead and keep up the Yanks   so it might follow up the troops with as much speed as possible. When we got within 800 yds. they opened terrifick fire of shot, shell, grape and cannister, and when the troops got to within 400 yds. the musketry united with cannon and it appeared to
came by the millions. I cannot see how any human being could live 2 moments in such a place. Our Division got to within a fiew steps of the works and some went upon them. Others could not get there for a thick hedge row of thorn bushes and after a little while the troops began to faulter and

were finally routed and came off in confusion, every man for himself. That is, those that were not killed or wounded. And here, Mary, I am so heart sick that I must stop writing for a while before I begin to tell of Dear friends that I have lost though I have nothing like a complete list . . .

Now, Mary, I will give you first a list of my Co. and then such others that I have heard of what you are acquainted with. The first is my lamented and never to be forgotten friend, Lieut. J. W. E. Spencer. He fell near the enemies works, shot through the stomach. I need not say a word to you in praise towards him for you know the kind feelings that has always existed between us. Lewis Thompson, an other good friend of mine, was killed, shot through the head.

Wounded, Jas. Vance severely in head, but I think there is a chance for him. David Anglin in the head, supposed to be mortally. John G. Neal, thigh broken. Sergt. G. W. Monts, little toe cut off and other mashed with fragment of shell, G. B. Cook, slightly in fore finger, R. P. Cochran, slightly bruised on foot, M. Norwood slightly on arm. The last three on the list are not hurt so as to cause them to quit the ranks. Co. D went in with 22 men. Capt. Marshall Rose is killed. Poor Marsh, I loved him. Elias Keeton wounded severely in neck, John Rogers killed, Capt. Thornton killed, Lieut. McLarty killed. John Gore, wounded in leg but walked off the field. I can not recollect all now and, in fact, I have not had time to see the different companies. Gen. Adams killed, Gen. Scott wounded, Gen. Clebourne killed, Col. Farrell mortally wounded. Walthall's Division went into the fight a fiew minutes after Loring and French soon after. Walthall's and all failed to carry the works. Cheatham carried his corps in about good dark and carried the enemies works, driving out of two lines of works.

The fight was kept up untill after midnight with terrible slaughter on both sides. The enemy finally abandoned the place and at day this morning they are all gone in the direction of Nashville and we are too badly crippled to follow. I do not know wheather Forrest is pursuing them or not.

    I have not been back to the battleground, but some of my men have and they say that it is horrible to behold. They are laying men in piles, some across others, and in some places the Yankees and Confederates are piled up together. The Yanks left their dead and severely wounded. We captured a good many prisoners but I do not know the number. Some say a Brigade.

    I have nearly rode the life out of my horse in the last fiew days. I will have to dispose of him now any way for I will have to take charge of Co. D for they have no officer now. Capt. Gilbert left us sick more than a month ago and has not returned yet. My Co. has been begging me to come back to them ever since I left them, and I have no excuse now to stay from them. Col. Stephens wounded, perhaps mortally. I learn that we march at 3 o'clock, I reckon on after the Yanks.

    Mary, give God the praise that I am still alive and well. Not a hair of my head was hurt. Not a thread of my clothing cut. Not even my horse was touched that I know of. I pray God to take care of you all and bring me safe home to you.

                            Your Husband,
                            W. H. Berryhill

Near Nashville, Tenn., Tuesday, Dec. 6, 1864

My Dear Wife,

    I finished a long letter at Franklin, Tenn., on last Thursday the 1st inst. but failed to get it off. Notwithstanding a mail went out the next day but I did not know of it until it was gone and I wouldn't have missed it for $5000. I felt somewhat let down when I found a mail had gone out and I was in the dark for I have generally beat everybody else on getting off letters. I have that letter on hand yet directed to Greensboro. I will direct this one to Bellefontaine and you will be shure to get one of them if they are ever mailed. I send them out by a negro that belongs to Lt. Col. Rorer of the 20th Miss. Regt. who was killed at Franklin. As I have given you a short account of each day since crossing the Tenn. River in the first letter, I will continue it in this.

    Thursday evening, the 1st Dec. After I closed my letter we moved out some 2 miles east of Franklin and the battle field and camped in the woods. The day had been spent in burying the dead and caring for the wounded. I did not see the field after the fight. I had to keep my place near HdQrs and do not know that I could have got permission to visit the field if I had asked it, and it was such an awful sight that I did not care much to look upon it, for the more of such sights a man sees the harder his heart becomes untill it becomes entirely frozen up to all feelings of humanity. My heart is already too hard.

    Friday the 2d. Began to rain before day. Took up the line of march for Nashville at sunrise, passed close in rear of this town. It appeared to be a very nice town situated on the banks of a large creek or small river which we had crossed the evening before. The town is on the south side but the Yanks had some of the strangest forts on the north side that I ever saw. I rode in to one that I saw firing into us during the fight, and this was the one that did us the most harm for I saw a many a shell burst in our midst that was thrown from it. I have never seen any work to equal it for strength or for its power for the destruction of assailants. The Yanks left some tremendous large cannons about these forts but they were spiked and the carriages cut down.

The rain fell slowly for half the day but we were on the Nashville turnpike which is the best road that you ever saw. So we reached to within 5 miles of Nashville long before night where Stewart's Corps left the pike and turned to the left and advanced to within some 3 miles of the City and formed in line of battle, for we found that the Yankees were in line some 2 miles this side of the City.

We moved first one way and then another untill after dark before we got in to position. We then camped the troops in line of battle mostly in a large cornfield. We camped near Gen. Loring's HdQrs in a woods or grass lot. We have plenty of wood but water is bad. We only have a small pond and men, horses, dogs and everything else are sloshing into it at will. We found a fiew dead Yanks on the road side which we buried. I picked up a good Hdkf with salt in it. I also picked up several gloves, one a splendid buck skin gauntlet, and a friend found a mate to it and gave it to me for $1.00, which made me a pair worth $20.00.

Saturday, the 3d. The lines advance some half mile to day and are skirmishing with the Yanks. I am still with the pioneer corps. Our camp has not been moved.

Sunday, Dec. 4th. No change since yesterday. Skirmishing continues. We are besieging the Yanks at Nashville now like they did us at Atlanta last summer. Forrest captured 2 transports on the Cumberland River below the City last night. He got some 60 prisoners and about 100 mules.

Monday, the 5th. Nothing worthy of note this day and every thing remains as yesterday so far as I know. The pioneers have not done a lick of work since we have been here, so you see we are getting well rested and out of reach of shot and shell, but in hearing of them.

Tuesday, the 6th. Is about as yesterday. Occasional sharpshooting is still going on. The Pioneers had to work for some batteries nearly all night last night and will have to work again tonight. I was a little unwell and did not go out but am better to day and will go with them to night. I have not been out of sight of camp since I have been here. I have had a spell of bowell complaint which is the first that I have had since crossing the Tenn. River. I have a strong apetite and eat too much is what brings it upon me.

There is more corn and fat hogs and cattle in this country than you ever saw. The people have not suffered as bad from the war here as they have where you are. And they sell cheaper for Confederate money here than they do in Miss. I bought some flour a fiew days ago at a little over 14 cts. or 7 lbs. to the dollar. Meal $2 per bushel and c. They will all tell you that they can not use Confederate money here, but still many of them will take it and at a much less rate than in Miss.

I have not seen my Co. to speak to them since the day after the fight. They are very anxious for me to come back to them, and Col. Harrison told me that he was going to make application to Gen. Loring to get me back to the command of Co. D, but I have heard nothing from it since leaving Franklin. I saw the Co. at a distance as we came up here and saw that Lieut. McCrary of Co. I was in command of it. He is a clever fellow and the boys like him, so I may not be ordered back. But he remains in command untill the Capt. returns. I have a good position here, but will make no effort to keep from going back to my Co. for the boys are all very kind to me and I love them and I believe they do me. They gave me the position of Lieut. during my absence and I must not neglect them. Poor fellows. When I saw them the next day after the fight with no officer they looked like lost sheep, and I felt as if I could have cryed my eyes out if it would have done any good. If you move to Bellefontaine and can get time, go to Uncle Billy Spencer and tell him how I loved Jimmy. I have known him from a small boy and never knew him to do a mean thing or verry from the truth.

I received a letter from Newton to day dated the 21st Nov. It came in 2 weeks which is pretty good considering the mail facilities in Tennessee. His letter said that the connections were all well except George who had taken down on his way back to his command. He was expected home the day he wrote. There may be letters for me with my Co. from you or Ira, as you both direct your letters there. Newt's was directed to the Pioneer Corps and came directly to HdQrs. I have sent a man to try to find my Co. to see if there is any thing from you. I have not been able to get but fiew more names of the killed and wounded of your acquaintances. Jim Latham shot through the arm. John Hitt killed and Robert Hitt mortally wounded. Zach Hannah and Jones were both badly wounded, Harris perhaps is dead. Our loss there in killed and wounded will not fall short of 4,000. I think the Yankee loss is at least 1,000 less than ours. May God bless and protect you. Pray for me.

Yours in Love,
W. H. Berryhill

This short undated note may not be in the proper order.

Gen. Hood says that he will take Nashville in 10 days. It is reported that Breckenridge is coming to form a junction with Hood here. If he does Nashville will fall. The Yanks have left Decatur and the Rail Road from there to Nashville is all in our hands, except 2 miles near Nashville. As soon as the road can be put in running order from Tuscumbia to Decatur we will have rail road communication to Corinth and from there to Mobile. It is reported here and believed that Sherman was whipped in Ga. and is in full retreat.

Billy

128

Nashville

In Front of Nashville, Tenn., Thursday, Dec. 8th, 1864

Dear Ira,

I have only 15 minutes to write and only do so to let you know that through the blessing of an alwise God I am still alive and in the enjoyment of a reasonable portion of health. I need not undertake to tell you about the great battle at Franklin, Tenn. for you will no doubt have heard of it before you get this. We drove the Yankees from the town but I feel shure that our loss was greater than theirs. I do not think that our loss will fall short of 4,000 in killed and wounded. I do not think that the Yankees loss will exceed 3,000. The Yanks carried the most of their wounded with them.

We lost 5 or 6 Generals, among them was Gen. Clebourne and Gen. Adams. Lieuts. J. W. E. Spencer and Lewis Thompson of my Co. were killed. They were both good friends of mine. I mourn their loss. David Anglin mortally wounded, John G. Neal thigh broken, J. A. Vance badly in head. They both may die. G. W. Monts slightly in foot, R. P. Cochran slightly bruised on foot, G. B. Cook slightly on finger, Norwood slight bruise on arm. The balance of my Co. are safe. Capt. Marshall Rose, Capt. Thompson and Lieut. McLarty killed, E. P. Keeton badly wounded in neck. John Hitt killed, Robert Hitt mortally wounded, John Gore in leg, Zain Latham through arm.

There was many others of your acquaintance but I can not now remember them and I have not been with the troops since the day after the fight. I will try to get a full list and send to you. Tell Mrs. Snow that Bud is safe and well.

I have just learned that the garrison at Murpheysboro has surrendered to our forces with 2,000 white men and 3 or 4,000 Negroes. I do not know the truth of the report.

Ira, I would write more but the mail is just in the act of starting. Write to me soon.

Your Brother,
W. H. Berryhill

P. S. It is very cold. The Battle at Franklin was fought on the 30 Nov.

LIEUT. WILLIAM HARVEY BERRYHILL
MAY 4, 1828 — DECEMBER 15, 1864

DIED — Lieut. Wm. H. Berryhill, Co. D, 43rd Miss. Regiment, who was killed at Battle of Nashville, Tenn. on the 15th of December, 1864.

He was born in Pickins County, Ala. May 4th, 1828 and migrated to Choctaw County, Miss. with his father and family in 1834. He was married in Oct. 1850 and leaves a wife and seven children to mourn their loss. He enlisted in May 1862 and was made orderly-sergeant. He was elected brevit second lieutenant in Oct. 1862 and was promoted to first lieutenant in the spring of 1863. He was in Vicksburg during the long and arduous siege of that city; was made prisoner with the rest of the garrison July 4th, and exchanged in November following General Polk's corps being ordered to Georgia. He arrived there in time to participate in the battle of Resaca.

He was soon after placed in command of the pioneer corps of Adams' Brigade, and on its discontinuance was made second in command of the division corps. He remained in the pioneer corps until a few days before the retreat from Nashville, when his old company, being without a commissioned officer, he returned to it and took command. While watching the movements of the enemy, he was shot through the head and expired about the time the retreat on that portion of our lines began.

In every position he held in the army, Lieut. Berryhill discharged his duties faithfully, won the love and respect of his subordinates, and the confidence and esteem of his superiors. He was a respectful and obedient son, a kind brother, an affectionate husband and father, a good citizen, a faithful soldier, and better than all, an humble follower of his Savior, having lived for years a pious and useful member of the Methodist Protestant Church.

*Rest, brother, in the
dreamless bed,
Where now thy body lies,
Till Christ, thy Savior,
wakes His dead
To meet Him in the skies.*

S. Newton Berryhill
Editor
Columbus, Miss. *Democrat*
Brother of W. H. Berryhill

THE BATTLE GROUND

Inscribed to the memory of my Brother, Lieut. Wm. H. Berryhill, Co. D, 43d Mississippi Regiment, who was killed at Nashville, Tennessee, December 15, 1864.

In memory of freedom's martyred dead
No monument we now may raise;
No sculptured marble at each soldier's head
May speak in coming years his praise.
But Spring, with noiseless step and face all sad,
Will robe with flowers each grassy mound,
And star-crowned Night, in mourning garments clad,
Will bathe in tears the holy ground.

No weeping nation now may come to chant
The funeral anthem of the brave,
Nor stricken loved ones seek the lonely haunt
To weep above the soldier's grave.
But wild free winds that through the forest sweep,
Will pause awhile their dirge to swell;
And moaning pines will midnight vigils keep
Above the spot where heroes fell.

The poet's lyre may never sound their fame,
Nor History's pen their deeds record;
And craven's tongues may load each hero's name
With epithets his soul abhorred.
But there are hearts—thank God! a chosen few—
Where still their memory is enshrined;
And deeds of men to duty ever true,
A lasting record there shall find.

—S. Newton Berryhill

I<small>N</small> ORDER TO GET THE LETTERS all down in one place, we are including the following pieces of letters which we were unable to put in their proper places. Some were pieces which had lost the top and bottom of the sheet, some had lost a side, some were front and back and some were written on the back of printed paper. But by placing them here, this means that everything that was in the little packet of letters that Mary Billy Miles kept for almost sixty years is here.

(BLUE SHEET — TORN — FRONT)

had heavy firing for
Our forces marched out
and charged the enemy and
their outer works to their
fortifications where our
brought to a standstill and firing
back to our fortifications.
very heavy. I saw scores upon
wounded in every conceivable
you can think of. Our b
directly in the charge
as a support and relieved those that first went into the fight. Our brigade had two or three men killed and ten or a doz. wounded and as many captured. I carried my corps in. I was put in on the right of the brigade and acted as a sort of separate command like a regt. There was no one hurt in my Corps. No body hurt in Co. D. Our Corps commander, Gen. Stewart, was wounded in the head. Gen. Cheatham commands in his place. Gen. Loring was . . .

THE GENTLE REBEL

(BLUE SHEET — BACK)

                              fight came off
                        some 3 miles from where
                   wrote you two days ago. Capt.
                   many others were left up there
                   have not been relieved yet
                   how they came out. I am
                   Yankees charged our pickets up
                   repulsed, charging an enemy
                   is a severe thing this going
                   of what the enemy have cost
                   charges upon our fortified
                              is still today up to this
hour [noon]. "A calm after a storm." Mary, I do not
know who is to carry this letter. I only know that a man is
going out. It may be the same that was to carry the others
not gone yet. I write often but think that you want to hear
often these dangerous times. If I only could get a letter from
you I might make one more interesting. I hardly think that
my corps will be put in an other fight for I was needed every
where else worse than there and had to leave my place and go
to Hd. Qrs. and else where several times during the time.
Trust in God and all will be well. Yours in Love,
                              W. H. Berryhill

(ONE SIDE OF FADED PAPER)

Camp near Union Ch. S. C., March 1st, 1865

ton Berryhill Dear Friend, I write you
w lines this evening mainly for the purpose
sending you a coppy of Billy's certificate
which you will please hand his

his wife. I have to
and may myself fall on some battle
and loose his as well as my own.

(AT BOTTOM OF SAME SHEET)

In Camp Lovejoy Station
Sept. 15, 1864

that I have this day paid W. H. Berryhill, 1st
D, 43rd Miss. Reg. Vols, Pay from Feb. 1, 1864
31st, 1864, inclusive.
$180.00   Signed Mj Jones, Pay & QM, Loring's
Division, Co. D, 43rd

(ON BACK OF THIS SAME SHEET)

Bryon I would write you a long letter
had time and was in a place that I could
with some   and it raining and
blanket. I wrote you while I was in the
       but did not get to mail it. Kept it
     then I tore it up. I suppose we
Charlotte, N.C., where it is thought that
and   man. I will not pr
       more. I know that this once as
army as the world ever saw is scattered
the four winds or left on the Battle field.
Convince the people that Gen. Johnston is

THE GENTLE REBEL

MRS. MARY ELIZABETH McDOWELL BERRYHILL

"My Dear Wife" with her grandson, Noel L. Miles, in one of the last pictures made before her death on February 9, 1921, while she was living with her daughter, Elizabeth Josephine Berryhill Miles, and "Lizzie's" daughter, Mary Billy. Noel, father and grandfather of the editors of *The Gentle Rebel*, died on June 5, 1983, after the first printing of the letters. He was 89, and very proud of this book and of "Ma Berryhill" — he remembered her so well and with such love.

136

APPENDIX I
FAMILY

MISS MARY BILLY MILES
December 10, 1889 — April 14, 1979

This book is more than just dedicated to Mary Billy Miles. It is hoped that it will be a sort of memorial to her memory. She was an unusual person — loved, admired, almost revered by those who knew her well, and instantly liked by those who came in contact with her only briefly. She touched many, many lives and left many grateful hearts.

We — her family — perhaps knew least of all the influence she had on the lives of others. She and her brother, Noel Miles, seldom lived in the same town, and somehow just occasional visiting does not provide time for observing daily living. She was, however, a very, very special person to her two nieces and, later, to all their children, and they shared a world of confidences and expectations, geared mostly to the present and the future.

After her death, and when we started working on these letters and family history, we found it rather ironic that most of the information we received had come from Mary Billy in the first place. We were gently chastised in one letter — "I am glad you are *finally* interested in your family history." We do regret that we didn't write down more of what Mary Billy told us, and that we did not spend more time talking about the past. But perhaps we can be forgiven this. In the times we spent together, frequent but often far too short, we were much too busy enjoying each other to be concerned about history!

Born on December 10, 1889, almost twenty-five years to the day after her grandfather died in the Battle of Nashville, Mary Billy Miles somehow became the mainspring of the entire W. H. Berryhill family. The second child of Elizabeth Josephine (Lizzie) Berryhill and Oliver Towles Miles, and one of only two who lived to maturity, she had an avid interest in everything and everybody. Her deep love for all members of that large Berryhill clan, coupled with a remarkable memory, made her the one to whom everyone came with their questions, their discoveries, their achievements, and she treasured them all, just as she treasured these letters from Billy Berryhill.

Teaching was surely the calling of Mary Billy Miles, but she readily admitted that she took her first teaching job, at age 16, because it paid more than the job she had in the telephone office!

Once begun, though, her teaching career spanned fifty-three years, and her rewards came from the achievements of her students. After her retirement she often noted that she had former students all the way from Alcatraz to Congress, and seemed to remember them all with the same degree of fondness. Mary Billy's relationship with her students in nearly all cases was a study in mutual love and understanding.

In her papers, which were in an old, scratched-up book satchel, there were copies of letters of recommendation that had been written in her behalf. These give some idea of her reputation as a person and as a school teacher:

. . . she is untiring in her efforts to build up the school and community. She makes her influence felt in the school room and also will do all in her power for the moral up-building of the community.

. . . she is conscientious, having the courage to stand by her convictions . . . is able to "hold her own" and handle problems arising in her department, and at the same time have her pupils with her. She is enthusiastic and ready to cooperate at all times.

. . . a highly cultured, sweet-spirited Christian, possessing the many virtues that constitute real moral worth and true womanhood. Her kind disposition and gentle manners give her easy access to the pupil's heart and when once won is forever held.

. . . is an excellent instructor and good disciplinarian . . . for the past three years she has done some very splendid work with her classes in the study of Sanitation and Personal Hygiene. This subject she has a unique way of handling which has proven to be very successful and which has excited some comment in the press and in educational journals.

. . . general letters of testimony are so easily procured and so often discounted on their face value that I feel that what I shall say in this will not convey my full meaning and do Miss Miles justice. For that reason, let me say that my interest in her is such and my confidence in her as a teacher and my regard for her as a Christian woman is so exalted that I shall be glad to confer personally, or communicate through personal letters, with any board of trustees before whom her application may come . . . level-headed . . .

excellent disciplinarian . . . full of common sense, good judgment and an unlimited supply of nerve . . . commands respect and esteem of all pupils . . . indefatiguable energy.

While some might say that Mary Billy was handicapped by poor vision, we would be hard pressed to find a time when she let her vision stand in the way of her accomplishing her desired task. Perhaps it was this independence, this determination, that kept us from realizing that there were so many more things she could have done had she had another pair of eyes at her disposal.

Many tributes and recognitions came her way during her long and successful life, but none that seemed to please her more than her last public appearance. One of her former pupils (the one in Congress!) asked her to introduce him at a homecoming in Eupora upon his retirement from the House of Representatives — on "Tom Abernathy Day." Mary Billy was approaching 80 years of age, and had almost completely lost her eyesight, but still had her "wits about her." She thoroughly enjoyed every moment of the day — from giving her well-received introduction, to beaming with pride at the praises heaped on the honored Tom Abernathy, to lunching at the big table with Congressman Abernathy, Senator John Stennis, Judge J. P. Coleman, and other dignitaries.

She thought it was splendid of a former student to share his day with his former teacher, making it sort of "her" day, too. She enjoyed the publicity and, we thought, almost stole the show!

Mary Billy Miles had a full, satisfying life, enriched by the love and dedication of all those who knew her and whose lives she, in turn, made more enjoyable, more productive, more satisfying. She died on April 14, 1979, in Yazoo City, Mississippi, with the same quiet dignity that had sustained her all through her life.

BERRYHILL/McDOWELL UNION

John Berryhill   John Portman   _____McDowell   _____Pierce
Martha_____   Katherine Cobb   _____   Gertrude Gilmore

Samuel BERRYHILL   *John McDOWELL*
married   *married*
Margaret (Peggy) PORTMAN   *Catherine Wiley PIERCE*

William Harvey BERRYHILL m. Mary Elizabeth McDOWELL
—THEIR CHILDREN AND GRANDCHILDREN—

Laura Newtonia — b. 9/24/1851 — d. 4/1929
married Nicholas Bethea Bridges
Alice, Robert Clifton, Noel Bernard, William Clinton,
Mary Birdeline, Loula Nichola, Claude, Edwin Roscoe,
and Laura Leola

Ira Jasper (Buddy) — b. 2/22/1855 — d. 2/3/1887
married Bertha Caldwell
One child who died in infancy

John Samuel — b. 4/24/1857 — d. after 1910
married Agnes Caldwell (sister of Bertha)
Homer Eldred, Mabel Claire, Rodrick Mortimer, Ira William,
John Wilbur, Roscoe Caldwell, Percy Claude, Lois Agnes,
Albert Herrick, and Herbert Woodrow

William Albert (Willie) — b. 8/29/1859 — d. 7/22/1950
married Julia Pierce
Mattie Lou and Ira Wesley

Martha Euphrasia Ann (Mattie) — b. 8/19/1861 — d. 8/14/1951
married Tom Smith
No children other than step-children

Elizabeth Josephine (Lizzie) — b. 3/29/1863 — d. 1/26/1946
married Oliver Towles Miles
Olive L., Annie Laura, Mary Billy, Ira Dell, Noel Lamar,
Oliver H., and Connie Zee

Mary Lula — b. 7/17/1864 — d. 9/20/1938
married Edwin Leslie Roberts
Oscar William, Myrtle, Ira May, Glyndon Eugene, Frank Leslie,
Mary Dell, Lula Berryhill, Jewell Gladys, and Edwin Lucille

BITS OF FAMILY HISTORY

THE LITTLE PIECES OF FAMILY history are included for our personal information and for other family members who may be interested. We know these things about the family and are just passing them on. We *think* that the Martha who married John Berryhill, and who was W. H. Berryhill's grandmother, was a full-blooded Creek Indian, but have not substantiated that yet.

NEWSPAPER OBITUARIES OF BERRYHILLS

DIED — Samuel Berryhill died at Bellefontaine, Mississippi, November 22, 1867, from a blow from a falling limb on the 12th. He was the son of John and Martha Berryhill and was born in Jasper County, Georgia, February 11, 1798. He came to Mississippi in 1820, settled in Columbus, married Margaret Portman on February 27, 1821. He moved to Pickens County, Alabama, and resided several years and then moved to Bellefontaine, Mississippi, in February, 1834. He was buried with Masonic honors.

DIED — At her residence in Bellefontaine, Choctaw County, Mississippi, on the 22nd day of February, 1873, Margaret Berryhill, daughter of John and Kathrine Portman, and widow of the late Samuel Berryhill.

Mrs. Berryhill was born in South Carolina in the year 1795, removed with her parents while an infant, to Kentucky, and subsequently to Tennessee; thence to Alabama. She was married to Samuel Berryhill in 1821, and settled the same year in Columbus, Mississippi, then a small hamlet. Subsequently she removed to Pickins County, Alabama, where she was converted to God in 1832, and joined the Baptist church. In 1834 she settled in Choctaw County, Mississippi, on the place where she died. Here she soon after joined the Methodist Church, of which she remained a faithful member. She was the mother of eight children, all of whom lived to maturity, but only four of whom survive her.

She was a good neighbor, and a kind affectionate Mother.

Mother, farewell; thy toil hath ended;
Sorrow and pain surcease have found;
And thou thy voice with saints hast blended
Where they the pure white throne surround.
SNB

(Both obituaries above were written by their son, S. Newton Berryhill.)

DIED — It becomes our sad duty to announce the death of one of our most distinguished citizens, S. N. Berryhill, which occurred at his residence, the old Berryhill Homestead, in Bellefontaine, on the 8th inst.

From his early youth he was a cripple and an invalid, but despite his physical infirmities he had achieved a name and reputation as a writer, a poet and a scholar that few men attain, though blessed with health, strength and opportunity for acquiring knowledge. This was the result of his own indomitable will, fine natural intellect and close application to his studies. Many years of his life were spent in teaching school and no teacher was ever beloved more by his students, and few were more successful than he in training the youthful mind.

Many of the readers of the *Warden* were once his pupils, to whom the news of his death will be a message of sadness. For some months prior to his demise, his always feeble body had been more than usually infirm, but the bright intellect shone on with undimished lustre to the last, sad day, when the unequal struggle with the Destroyer was over and his body was committed to the dust at the North Union graveyard.

An immense concourse of friends assembled there to do the last sad honor to their loved neighbor. Eloquent speeches were made by Rev. A. B. Hicks and Prof. W. J. Taylor, and few were the dry eyes in that large audience when all that was mortal of S. Newton Berryhill was lowered to its final resting place. The spirit of one so pure, so gifted, so unselfish, can scarcely fail of acceptance in that land "where the wicked cease from troubling, and the weary are at rest."

DIED — Dr. William Albert Berryhill was born on August 29, 1859, at Old Greensboro, the son of William Harvey and Mary Elizabeth McDowell Berryhill, and the old home place in which he was born is still standing at Old Greensboro. (This was written on July 27, 1950.)

His paternal grandparents were Samuel and Margaret Portman Berryhill, a daughter of John Portman, a revolutionary soldier in Georgia who came to Mississippi via Alabama, living for a time at the present site of Columbus, Mississippi, where twins, George, one time Eupora postmaster, and Jeff Berryhill, who died in early manhood, were born, being the first white children born in that area. The family returned to Pickens County, Alabama, where William Harvey Berryhill was born on May 4, 1828.

The next westward move brought the Berryhill family to Bellefontaine in Webster County (then Choctaw County), known for a long time as Berryhill Town. The Berryhill brothers opened a cabinet shop, and the brothers George, John, and Billy built homes near Father Samuel's which stood about where the Reverend J. V. Wilson's beautiful brick house now stands. Many chests, cabinets and tables from this shop may still be found in the county.

His maternal grandparents were John McDowell and Katy Pierce McDowell, a close relative of the early Methodist preacher, Lovick Pierce. They lived in North Carolina and for awhile Mr. McDowell taught school in Alabama and then the family came to Mississippi by the route through Columbus, which by that time boasted of a tavern and a grocery. Finally they joined friends to make their home in Calhoun County and with other pioneer families lived in "lean to's" until the houses could be built. Mr. McDowell continued his pedagogical practices for many years after coming to Mississippi. Politically he was progressively Whig and Unionist, but was able to accept with complete understanding the Congregationist and ardent Democrat.

William Albert Berryhill was the fourth child of the McDowell-Berryhill union. Hence when the Yankees came just nine days after his father had died leading a charge at Nashville, Tennessee, for States' Rights, he was only five years old. But he considered himself a person of great importance that day because while his elder brothers were searched by the soldiers, his own pockets bulged with all the family fortune in Confederate money. That was but the first of a long series of responsibilities for William Albert Berryhill. Christmas Day in 1864 dawned on a Berryhill home with the whole harvest either carried away or destroyed, nothing left but a roof and a young widow who had not yet learned of her bereavement, with her seven orphans ranging in age from thirteen years to five months.

NEWSPAPER ARTICLES

The following article was published in the *Walthall Warden*, newspaper in Choctaw (later Webster) County, Mississippi. It was written by S. Newton Berryhill, brother of William Harvey Berryhill and had evidently been printed prior to this printing. S. Newton Berryhill died in 1887.

OUR PIONEERS

The following appeared in the Walthall Warden several years ago and will be of interest to many of our readers:

"The advanced age attained by the early settlers of a country are indicative of its healthfulness. In this respect few counties can make a better showing than ours.

"The first settlements were made in the county in 1833. The persons I shall name came to the county prior to 1839.

"**John Portman**, who came in 1834, died in 1857, aged 90 years. Coleman M. Roberts, who came in 1833, died last year, aged 85. Mrs. Jennie Castles died four years ago, aged about 90. Lawrence Latham, who came in 1833, died about three years ago, aged 86. **Samuel Berryhill**, who came in 1834, was killed by a falling limb in 1867, aged 70. **Margaret Berryhill**, his wife, died in 1873, aged 78.

"Benjamin Middleton died in 1881, aged about 90. His brothers, John and Parks, died before the war, having passed their seventieth year.

"These have died since the war, aged 80 years and upwards: Jacob Starnes, Charles M. Holland and his wife, Absalom Holland, Mrs. Jemima McQuary, Mrs. Prudence Morris, William Castles, Thomas Fox, Joseph Fox, David Lovett, Wm. G. Childress, William Spencer, Gideon Watson, Charles Cox, and **Mrs. Katie McDowell.**

"Ezekiel Langston, who came in 1833, died about six years ago over seventy years of age. His widow, Mrs. Polly Langston, is still alive and has passed her 74th year. Francis B. Campbell, who came in 1834, went to Texas a few years ago and is still alive. He is about 80 years old. **John McDowell** is 80 years old; Silas Watson is 82; Judge Snow, James Moore, Gilbert Coffy and Judge Davis, each over 75; Allen Moore, Rev. B. Watson, Rev. J. B. Burson, John Tharp, Toliver Keeton (now of Grenada County) each over 70.

"Mrs. W. G. Childress is still alive, and is over 80. Terrell Rose, a pioneer of 1833, the first man who ever married in the county, is past 72, and with his wife still lives within a mile of the place where they were married nearly a half century ago.

"If the writer has made any mistakes in what he has written, he would thank some old citizen to correct him through the Warden. He would also thank any one to furnish him through the same medium with any names omitted of persons who came to the county prior to 1839 and died at an advanced age.

"S. NEWTON BERRYHILL."

HAND-ME-DOWN FAMILY STORIES

As told by George W. Berryhill and his nieces and nephews to Mary Billy Miles

*****

John Portman
Samuel and Margaret (Peggy) Portman Berryhill
Brother Jeff takes Newt to school
Billy goes to a "dumb supper"
Sally Ann pays a visit to Greensboro
George talks politics
The school master
S. Newton and the children
Grand pap's salesmanship
W. H. buys a slave
A tragic Christmas story

A typewritten sheet among Mary Billy Miles's papers carried the above beginning of "Hand-Me-Down Family Stories." Only the following report about John Portman was on the sheet. What happened to the other stories she wrote — if she ever got them down — is a mystery.

The other stories in this section are reconstructed from the memories of Leslie Martin, Jewel Roberts, Noel Miles and Mary Miles Jones. Jewel and Noel heard them from Mary Elizabeth Berryhill and others; Leslie and Mary heard them only from Mary Billy. We believe the situations and outcomes are correct, but some of the details may not be. The information about the McDowell family came from Wendell and Mattie McDowell, who spent many hours with Mary Billy Miles many years ago.

JOHN PORTMAN

John Portman seems to have been a typical frontiersman, making his way over not-so-well beaten paths from South Carolina to Mississippi via Georgia and Kentucky. In fact, his family seemed imbued with the same spirit for there is no record in family annals that his wife, Mary Cobb Portman, hesitated to bundle up their offspring and hit the trail any time passports to trading points in

Georgia, Kentucky, or Mississippi were issued. There was no record of sons in their family, but the four daughters grew to womanhood.

Grand Daddy Portman, as he was known to his grandchildren and close associates, remained hale and hearty to within a week of his death. Two or three weeks before he died, he walked a mile to the home of his grandson, spent an hour or two playing with the children, told them stories of his life on the trail, and then walked a mile back to his daughter Peggy's home. He told her he would not likely do as much walking in one day again.

It was the last time he ever left home. They buried him in North Union Cemetery, Bellefontaine, Mississippi, building a brick house over the grave with a stone marker in one end showing his dates beneath a masonic emblem.

The house has crumbled in recent years and the stone is broken, but the world can still see that a gallant old Mason lies there.

*****

W. H. BUYS A SLAVE

Billy and Mary Berryhill did not own slaves, except for the unusual circumstances related in this story which was told many times by Mary Billy Miles, but which we failed to write down. The thought and intent of the story is true, although the details may not be entirely accurate. For instance, we do not know who owned the slave whose husband was being auctioned off on the slave block.

What we do know is that the man, when sold, would probably go away from his wife, and she was very upset about it. Billy Berryhill was at the auction. When the man appeared on the block to be sold, the woman went to her knees in front of Billy and, clutching his legs, begged, "Bid, Massa Billy, bid!" He did bid, and each time the bid went higher the woman would shout, "Bid, Massa Billy, bid!" He finally outbid everyone, bought the man and, apparently, since there is never any mention of owning a slave in the letters, freed him.

Noel Miles remembers that there was an old black woman who worked for them when he was a child. She was almost blind, and hard of hearing, but they all loved Harriet. Perhaps Harriet was the woman in this story.

BILLY GOES TO A "DUMB SUPPER"

One of the most popular parties for young adults of courting age during the mid-1800's was the "dumb supper." The name of the party was derived, apparently, from the fact that the girls were to gather at someone's house and prepare a meal in complete silence. Questions such as "Have the beans been salted?" or "How long should this meat be cooked?" could not be asked. The girls also could not discuss current events, the weather, or—hardest of all—they could not say a word about the young men waiting outside for invitations to supper.

When the meal was ready, each girl would write out an invitation and tie it to a rock with a long string attached. The girls would then throw the rocks out an open window in the direction of the young men. Each young man would pick up a rock, and the girls would pull in their escort for the evening.

One such supper occurred in the summer of 1850. Billy Berryhill was one of the young men gathered outside a house where several girls were trying to prepare a meal in silence. Billy let it be known among his friends that he wanted to be Mary McDowell's escort—and not for just that one evening. He enlisted their help in letting him catch the rock that she threw when supper was ready. He was Mary's date for that evening, and proposed to her that night.

When they were married on October 17, 1850, he gave her a locket rather than a wedding ring. The locket is one of Leslie Martin's proudest possessions.

A TRAGIC CHRISTMAS STORY

The Union Army, represented by General Benjamin Grierson, came through Choctaw County on December 24, 1864, burning most of the homes in Old Greensboro and destroying everything of value to the women and children in the county.

Mary Berryhill was milking their lone cow when she saw the Yankees approaching. Hurrying into the house where she lived with her seven children and one servant, she made quick decisions. She took a ham that was curing, dumped the precious salt on the ground right outside the back door and trampled it into the ground out of sight. Then she sent her oldest daughter, Laura, and the servant woman to a ditch behind the house, carrying the ham they planned to subsist on for some time.

THE GENTLE REBEL

Hoping that he would be too young to arouse suspicion, Mary selected five-year-old Willie to carry their money. She stuffed his pants pockets with all the coins and bills they had in the house.

There was a hole in the floor under a rug, and into this Mary put what things she could get her hands on in the few minutes she had. She later remembered, and her children and grandchildren enjoyed her smile when she told it, that the only thing she could remember stuffing in the hole was her favorite bonnet! Then she laid the rug back over the hole, sat her churn on the rug, and was preparing to strain her fresh milk into the churn when the Yankees burst in.

Within a short time the troops had destroyed everything the family owned. Dishes were broken; pillows, mattresses, and linens were slashed with swords; sacks of flour and meal were ripped open and poured out; family records were torn out of the Bible; and all their furniture was piled under the front porch so that a fire could be started easily and the house could be burned to the ground.

At one point during all this, several Yankees drank Mary's unstrained milk, and she was able to voice her contempt and indignation when she muttered, "Well, I thought you were hogs — now I know it!"

During all of this commotion, young Willie became extremely upset. One of the Union soldiers picked him up and rocked him in a chair in front of the fireplace. It is not known whether the soldier simply did not relize that the boy was carrying the family's money, or if he felt the coins and bills in Willie's pants and decided to remain silent. We like to think that it was the latter.

As the army prepared to leave, they began setting fires to burn the house. Mary begged the commanding officer to spare her home, saying that a roof over their heads would be all that she would be able to give her children for Christmas. Three-year-old Mattie, who was born with a winning personality and plenty of spunk, interceded also, stepping forward and putting her foot down at burning her house, and charming completely the Union soldiers. Only one fire—one under the front porch—was set, and it was quickly extinguished by the family after the troops had left.

They saved their lives, their house, their Confederate money, their cured ham, and Mary's favorite bonnet. It was several days before they learned of their most devastating loss — that of their husband and father, ten days before Christmas, in the Battle of Nashville, Tennessee.

ABOUT JOHN McDOWELL AND HIS SON, IRA McDOWELL

John McDowell was a Whig—a Union man. He did not believe in secession and neither did his son, Ira McDowell. Ira was a firm believer in States' Rights, but not in secession, so he did not join others from Choctaw County who served with the Confederate Army.

At one time during the war—probably in 1862 or 1863—the Confederate Army sent troops to arrest Ira because he would not fight. He was tried under General Featherston, but the case was thrown out of court.

Ira McDowell was probate clerk during the war and later was appointed by Governor Ames as president of the Board of Supervisors of Webster County, which was formed out of Choctaw.

John McDowell had a red-haired brother named Harvey. John left his home near Raleigh, North Carolina, because his mother would not let him marry the girl of his choice. John's father came from Ireland, and the family members were Quakers. John's grandfather was from Scotland. His mother was born on the ocean voyage to America.

If these stories stir the memories of anyone who has heard them before, especially anyone who can recall the ones listed on Page 145 which we have no record of, please contact Leslie Martin, 107 Dundee Drive, Natchez, Mississippi 39120.

FROM THE W.P.A. PROJECT, History of Webster County, Mississippi, there is taken the following item:

"About 1830, Berryhill town, Mississippi, now known as Bellefontaine, Mississippi, was established near the Old Indian Battleground where the Chicksaws and Choctaws combined and extinguished the whole of the Choctuma race. At the advent of a sawmill, and the establishment of a Male & Female High School, this little village reached its peak."

APPENDIX II
CO. D, 43rd REGIMENT

BECAUSE OF THE LOVE AND RESPECT that W. H. Berryhill had for all the men of Co. D, 43rd Regiment, we are printing below a list of the men of Co. D which was with Mary Billy Miles' papers. The list was probably made before the surrender at Vicksburg, and is by no means a complete list of all who served at one time or another with Co. D.

Captain Thomas B. Thompson
Lieutenant J. Gilbert
Lieutenant J. W. E. Spencer
Lieutenant Sam DeLoach
Orderly Sergeant W. H. Berryhill

G. W. Berryhill	O. Clegg	W. Morris	J. Randle
R. Thompson	J. Orst	N. F. Ray	F. Swindle
L. Thompson	J. Norris	W. A. Ray	J. Bingham
J. Thompson	Arnolds (2)	W. Croley	H. Marks
Z. Lamb	J. Hruckaba	J. Croley	J. P. Elkins
M. Lamb	E. Hruckaba	J. Gilbert	D. Gore
H. Lamb	J. L. Norwood	G. Branch	J. Jones
J. Lamb	J. M. Norwood	M. Branch	J. Adair
W. Lamb	F. Alexander	W. C. Sugg	T. T. Smith
E. Lamb	J. J. Carroll	G. McTombs	G. W. Oswalt
J. Hufman	Tom Carroll	J. Watson	J. F. Dunlap
M. C. Moore	G. B. Cook	J. McAllister	D. Ferguson
W. Moore	N. Summers	J. Collins	W. Farmer
J. Klutts	D. Morris	Stanford	Tom Lamb
G. Monts	Kirk Morris	Stanford	R. P. Cochran
G. Clegg			

There is an account of the 43rd Regiment in the *Military History of Mississippi,* Dunbar Rowland, and military records can be obtained from the Mississippi and the National Archives. The only other account we found of Co. D was a report written by T. T. Smith[1] on February 17, 1899. This report was presented to the Mississippi Department of Archives and History by Mrs. Barbara Peacock, Salisbury, North Carolina.

---

1. Smith (Thomas) Manuscript
    February 17, 1899 (photostat copy of typewritten manuscript).
    Mississippi Department of Archives and History. Z 762 f.

APPENDIX III
S. NEWTON BERRYHILL
The Backwoods Poet

DR. W. CLYDE SNOW, DESCENDANT of Martha Berryhill Snow who was a sister of W. H. and S. Newton Berryhill, published two volumes of the words of S. Newton Berryhill. The first was a reprint of *Backwoods Poems,* which was published in the late 1800's, and the other was a collection of writings, by the poet and by others who wrote about him.

Dr. Snow, who lived in Ralls, Texas, was a retired physician who spent the last decade of his life collecting this information to give an insight into the life of S. Newton Berryhill.

As an addition to the information in those books, we have secured permission to reprint the first edition of the Mississippi Historical Society's newsletter, dated June, 1898, which was about S. Newton Berryhill. We have omitted most of the portions of his poems which were mentioned in this article, since all the poems are in Dr. Snow's books. We believe that the information about the education and rearing of S. Newton Berryhill casts some light on the early childhood and upbringing of W. H. Berryhill, who was four years older than S. Newton Berryhill.

PUBLICATIONS
OF THE
MISSISSIPPI HISTORICAL SOCIETY

VOL. I	JUNE, 1898	NO. 1

MISSISSIPPI'S "BACKWOODS POET."
BY DABNEY LIPSCOMB, A. M.

To awaken greater interest in what, however estimated, Mississippians have accomplished in the field of literature, to provoke research into even its remote and unfrequented corners; and, chiefly, to place more prominently before the people of his much-loved State a poet too little known, is the double purpose of this essay.

The poet needs no introduction and offers no apology on his entrance into the domain of history; for he is no intruder there, entitled indeed to a place of honor in the proudest capitol of that noble realm. Homer precedes Herodotus and makes his record doubly valuable. The poet is in fact the maker in large measure of the history of the world. Through his entrancing and inspiring voice the aspirations of humanity have been elevated, ideals lofty in thought and deed have been constantly upheld, and will to dare and do the utmost in the cause of liberty and righteousness

THE GENTLE REBEL

has been imparted in the hour of need. In the poet's verse we read, as nowhere else, the inner throbbing life of man. High or low his ascent of Parnassus, his words have a charm for us, if the Muse has bidden him welcome; and the nearer he is to us the more apt he will be to express our peculiar griefs and joys in his melodious strains.

Hence, it is with pleasure, that the claims of Mississippi's "Backwoods Poet" to our affection and appreciation are now presented. Perhaps, he is not the greatest of the thirty or forty that might be named who in our State have as poets achieved more or less local distinction. He modestly disclaimed such honor, and assumed himself the title of "Backwoods Poet" which has been given him. S. Newton Berryhill, of Choctaw (now Webster) County, Mississippi, is his proper name. He was born October 22, 1832, and died December 8, 1887.

In the preface of his poems these significant facts are stated:

While I was yet an infant, my father with his family settled down in a wilderness, where I grew up with the population, rarely ever going out of the neighborhood for forty years. The old log school house, with a single window and a single door, was my alma mater, the green woods was my campus.

Yet what he learned in the log school house and the woods and by subsequent private study would put to shame very many who have enjoyed far better educational advantages; especially, when the further disadvantage under which he labored is considered. Early in life he became invalid, unable the remainder of his days to stand upon his feet. Despite all these, to an ordinary man, crushing limitations, he became fairly proficient in Latin, French, German, and music, in addition to a thorough knowledge of the usual high school courses in English, science, and mathematics.

To teaching, journalism, and literature he devoted his life. After a long and creditable career as teacher near his country home, during which time most of his poetry was written, he moved, about 1875, to Columbus, Mississippi. In the dingy office of the old *Columbus Democrat,* the writer first saw this unquestionably remarkable man. Cushioned in his wheel chair, before a desk, busy with his pen, Mr. Berryhill, the editor, saw not how closely he was observed, nor the look of pity he might have read in his beholder's face for one so handicapped in the race of life. But as the massive, thinly covered head was raised, and the dauntless, lofty spirit of the man shone from the dark and deep-set eyes; as the almost cheerful expression of his pallid countenance was revealed,—pity gave way to wonder and admiration, which grew yet more with further knowledge of the man and his achievements against odds apparently so overwhelming. How respectfully on bright Sundays when he could venture out, he was lifted in his chair by friends up the double flight of steps to the audience room of the church and rolled down the aisle to the place near the pulpit, sympathetic glances following him the while, is a picture, too, not soon to be forgotten.

During his stay in Columbus he was elected County Treasurer, which office he filled acceptably two years. In 1880 he returned to Webster county, where, as has been stated, he died, December 8, 1887. Little else, for the lack of information, except that he was a Methodist and a Mason, can be said of the life and character of Mr. Berryhill. What more is given must be gathered from his writings in an inferential way, which for this purpose and for their literary merit, will repay the examination now proposed.

The editorials, sound, progressive, and patriotic, must be laid aside. The rather crude but racy character sketches, Indian legends, and miscellaneous short stories, written in part during his quiet closing years, must, also, more regretfully be left unnoticed for lack of time. His poetry is the work he prized most highly, and by it his place in literature should be determined.

From boyhood, he was irrepressibly poetic. The spirit of the woods and hills early descended on him, giving his eye unwonted keenness in discerning the beauty that surrounded him, and his ear unwonted delicacy in detecting the melody that floated in every breeze. Romantic stories of their better days told him by neighboring friendly Choctaws took deep root in his youthful fancy and bore fruit in his prose and verse.

In 1878 his poems written during the forty years previous were published at Columbus in a volume entitled "Backwoods Poems." Political issues of very serious nature, not altogether settled, were then too absorbing a theme to Mississippians to permit them to pay much heed to poetry, however excellent. Hence, the work received less notice than otherwise it would. But one edition was ever published, and few copies of it can now be found.

What first strikes the reader as he turns the pages of this unpretentious little volume is the variety and uniform excellence of the versification. Under the circumstances, it was natural to suppose that this poet would attempt little else than the rhyming couplet and the ballad form of verse. Instead, stanzas varying greatly in length and rhyme order, with lines from two to six stresses, iambic and often trochaic in movement, usually well sustained, soon make a strong impression that no common poetaster has set the music to these verses.

As to length, not more than half a dozen of the two hundred twenty-six poems in the collection contain more than one hundred lines. The longest and leading poem, called Palila, is a metrical version of a favorite Choctaw legend, numbering one thousand tetrameter lines. This pathetic story of an Indian maiden and her ill-starred gallant lover and the upshooting by the medicine spring of the little flower the pale-face calls the lady's slipper, but known to red men as Palila's Moccasin, is told with dramatic effect, and has the atmosphere of freedom and wildness befitting a tale so weird and sad. Bare mention of two or three other rather lengthy poems, such as "A Heart's History," and "The Vision of Blood," will be made, principally to call attention to the excellence of the blank verse in which they are written; its ease, accuracy, and vigor are readily perceived.

The shorter poems may be conveniently classed as anacreontic, humorous, patriotic, descriptive, and personal. Many of them, as the author admits, especially those of his youth, are crude and imperfect, but he explains in a personally suggestive way that he could not cast out these poor children of his brain on account of their deformity, and craves indulgence where approval or applause must be withheld.

The poems of love and humor have little value except for the light they throw on the poet, who, though deprived of nearly all the heart holds dear in life, could yet fully sympathize with youth in its joys and smile genially even on its follies.

* * * * *

"The Vision of Blood" written in 1864 is too long, and even if not, too lurid in its imagery to justify reproduction now. Instead let us take this glimpse into those days of death and disaster to the South:

(The one verse quoted from "Tidings From the Battlefield" had reference to Mary Elizabeth McDowell Berryhill after she learned of the death of her husband.)

THE GENTLE REBEL

TIDINGS FROM THE BATTLEFIELD
* * * * *

"Fresh tidings from the battle field!"
  The wife her needle plies,
While in the cradle at her feet
  Her sleeping infant lies.
"Fresh tidings from the battle field!"
  "Your husband is no more,
But he died as soldiers love to die,
  His wounds were all before."
Her work was dropped—"O God" she moans,
  And lifts her aching eyes;
The orphaned babe in the cradle wakes,
  And joins its mother's cries.

* * * * *

But it is in the poems personal and descriptive that we get close to this poet's heart. There will be found what gave most solace to his circumscribed and lonely life. In nature as she was most attractive to him, and in lines to loved ones young and old, plaintive often but never rebellious or morose, the placid, self-restrained, yet inspiring nature of the man is brought to clearest view. Fervid in his love for beauty, he bowed none the less devoutly at the shrine of duty.

* * * * *

Perhaps Mr. Berryhill's best known poem is one that is personal and yet quite fanciful. It can be found in Miss Clarke's "Songs of the South." Two or three stanzas will be sufficient:

MY CASTLE
They do not know who sneer at me because I'm poor and lame,
And round my brow has never twined the laurel wreath of fame—
They do not know that I possess a castle old and grand,
With many an acre broad attached of fair and fertile land;
With hills and dales, and lakes and streams, and fields of waving grain,
And snowy flocks, and lowing herds, that browse upon the plain.
In sooth, it is a good demesne—how would my scorners stare,
Could they behold the splendors of my castle in the air!

* * * * *

The banks may break, and stocks may fall, the Croesus of today
May see, tomorrow, all his wealth, like snow, dissolve away.
And the auctioneer, at panic price, to the highest bidder sell
His marble home in which a king might well be proud to dwell.
But in my castle in the air, I have a sure estate
No panic with its hydra head can e'er depreciate.
No hard-faced sheriff dares to levy execution there,
For universal law exempts a castle in the air.

Little remains to be said. This singular life, with an estimate of the quality and quantity of its work has been unfolded as faithfully as possible.

With greater interest, the dominant motive of the author, so frankly stated, may now be joined, without comment, to his mournful retrospect of his life work. The first is found in the lines from Mrs. Hemans inscribed on the title page of "Backwoods Poems."

————I'd leave behind
Something immortal of my heart and mind.

This is his salutatory. In the closing stanza of the last poem, "Unfinished," the retrospect is made and his valedictory delivered thus:

My canvas is not full; a vacant space
Remains untouched. To fill it were not meet—
I'll leave it so—like all that bears a trace
Of me on earth—Unfinished—incomplete.

To Hayne, Lanier, and Maurice Thompson, S. Newton Berryhill must yield in subtlety of melody and penetrative insight into nature's deeper meanings. Timrod and Ticknor in their war lyrics may, at times, have struck the martial chord with stronger and more dextrous hand; but it may still be justly claimed that the best of the "Backwoods Poems" compare favorably with much or even most of the work of these more famous Southern poets.

If in this paper this claim has been established, its purpose is abundantly fulfilled, and the "Backwoods Poet" in environment and achievement stands out a unique figure in the literature of the State.[1]

---

1. "Mississippi's 'Backwoods' Poet," by Dabney Lipscomb, p. 1-15, Mississippi Historical Society, *Publications,* Volume I. Reprinted by permission of the Mississippi Department of Archives and History and the Mississippi Historical Society.

INDEX
OF NAMES MENTIONED IN THE LETTERS

(The names are given just as they are in the letters. We have made no attempt to determine correct first or last names, even of the officers who are well known.)

A
Adams, Gen. — 35, 37, 38, 50, 56, 57, 61, 63, 94, 123, 129
Anglin, David — 40, 123, 129
Armstrong, _____ — 95

B
Banks, Col. — 16
Bates, _____ — 29
Beauregard, Gen. — 105
Bennett, Stephen — 104
Berryhill, Emma — 87, 90, 91, 94
Berryhill, Elizabeth J. (Lizzie) — 34, 44, 73, 97, 100
Berryhill, George — 4, 18, 23, 34, 40, 44, 50, 56, 57, 61, 65, 66, 71, 79, 87, 88, 93, 94, 102, 111
Berryhill, Ira J. (Buddy) — 18, 56, 67, 68, 69, 73, 74, 79, 90
Berryhill, John Samuel — 20, 56, 115
Berryhill, John Wesley — 4, 5, 54
Berryhill, Laura — 10, 40, 44, 54, 58, 67, 68, 69, 71, 74, 87, 89, 90, 94, 97, 108
Berryhill, Martha (Mattie) — 10, 19, 97, 100, 103
Berryhill, Mary Lula — 97, 100
Berryhill, S. Newton — 4, 44, 54, 66, 67, 68, 69, 73, 74, 79, 87, 89, 90, 91, 92, 94, 103, 109, 115, 128
Berryhill, William Albert (Willie) — 56, 115
Brantley, Gen. — 65, 114
Breckenridge, _____ — 128
Bridges, Estus — 39
Bryon, _____ — 90
Buford, _____ — 71

C
Caldwell, Bland — 18, 39, 40, 50, 72
Campbell, Jas. N. — 45
Capps, _____ — 40, 102
Cheatham, Gen. — 107, 110, 111, 123, 133
Clark, John — 27
Clebourne, Gen. — 28, 32, 123, 129
Clegg, James — 51
Cochran, R. P. — 51, 123, 129
Cochran, Tom — 51
Conner, Hubbard — 68, 69
Cook, Bob O. — 51, 71, 111
Cook, G. B. — 123, 129
Corbett, Major — 8, 9

D
Davis, _____ — 51
Davis, Pres. Jefferson — 9, 57
Davis, Lt. John B. — 42
Drane, Col. — 60

E
Embry, _____ — 41

F
Farmer, W. H. — 18, 40
Farrell, Col. — 86, 88, 123
Featherston, Gen. — 19, 23, 38, 46, 47, 60, 62, 64
Forrest, Gen. — 18, 47, 53, 71, 117, 118, 119, 124, 126
French, Gen. — 45, 123
Fry, Lt. — 86

G
Gilbert, Capt. J. — 19, 39, 58, 61, 104, 124
Gilbert, Thomas — 39, 51
Golding, Jo — 104
Gore, James — 90
Gore, John — 123, 129
Gore, Notley — 36
Gore, Owens — 67, 69
Grandberry, Gen. — 32
Grant, Gen. — 53
Green, _____ — 51
Green, Gen. — 4

H
Hannah, Zach — 128
Hardee, Gen. — 26, 45, 47, 48, 49, 62, 91, 95, 107
Harris, Charles — 40
Harris, _____ — 128
Harrison, Col. — 37, 127
Harvey, Eugene — 51, 60
Harvey, Tom — 51
Hitt, John — 128, 129
Hitt, Reuben — 43
Hitt, Robert — 128, 129
Holloway, Frank — 64, 114
Holmes, Arch — 16, 39, 40, 51, 71

Hood, Gen. — 26, 38, 58, 71, 81, 93, 101, 104, 105, 128

J
Jackson, Gen. — 65, 66, 95
Johnson, W. L. — 30
Johnston, Gen. Joe — 26, 27, 28, 29, 34, 40, 43, 46, 50, 53, 57, 71, 91
Jones, _____ — 128

K
Keeton, Elias P. — 123, 129
Keneda, David — 40
Klutts, J. — 40

L
Lamb, Haze — 51
Latham, Henry — 105, 116
Latham, Jim (Zain) — 128, 129
Lee, Gen. — 95, 106, 107, 109, 110
Loring, Gen. — 19, 32, 38, 39, 43, 47, 49, 56, 57, 62, 64, 67, 96, 123, 126, 127, 133

Mc
McBryde, Jo — 4
McCain, B. F. (Frank) — 39, 51, 71, 102, 115, 116
McCrary, Lt. — 127
McDowell, Mr. — 90
McDowell, Ada — 110
McDowell, Ira — 8, 9, 18, 23, 34, 49, 54, 57, 70, 79, 97, 103, 109, 110, 129
McLarty, Lt. — 103, 105, 123, 129
McPherson, Gen. — 62
McVey, _____ — 39, 51

M
Martin, _____ — 79, 81
Massey, Maj. — 47
Middleton, Capt. — 51
Monts, George W. — 102, 123, 129
Moore, Allen — 73, 82
Moore, D. — 39, 51

N
Neal, John G. — 123, 129
Nolen, _____ — 9
Norris, J. A. — 40
Norwood, J. M. — 95
Norwood, M. — 123, 129

O
Oswalt, George — 22, 39
Oswalt, Medy — 60

P
Parker, Lt. — 51, 65
Polk, Gen. — 26, 43, 45, 46, 118
Prewitt, Capt. — 79
Price, Gen. (Pap) — 4
Proctor, _____ — 72

R
Randle, Capt. — 86
Randle, Jim — 51
Rasberry, _____ — 69
Reynolds, _____ — 60
Rogers, John — 123
Rorer, Lt. Col. — 125
Rose, Marshall — 57, 103, 123, 129
Ruddy, Gen. — 66
Ruggles, Gen. — 16

S
Scott, _____ — 38, 48
Scott, Gen. — 123
Shaw, _____ — 34
Sherman, Gen. — 46, 48, 52, 53, 62, 75, 76, 81, 82, 88, 101, 123
Smith, Kirby — 53
Smith, T. T. — 18
Smith, Truss — 51, 102, 111
Snow, Appalona — 87, 91, 94
Snow, Mrs. and Bud — 10, 62, 130
Spencer, Albert — 119, 122
Spencer, Lt. J.W.E. — 16, 39, 61, 64, 66, 122, 123, 128, 129
Spencer, Levi — 40
Spencer, Marion — 61
Spencer, Uncle Billy — 128
Stewart, Gen. — 43, 50, 95, 107, 110, 111, 126, 133
Stone, Chaplain — 37
Sweatman, David L. — 65, 66, 114
Sykes, Adj. — 103, 105
Sykes, Col. — 32, 45, 103

T
Tharp, _____ — 61
Thompson, Bill — 73
Thompson, Lewis — 51, 71, 123, 129
Thompson, Capt. — 72, 129
Thornton, Capt. — 60, 105, 116, 123
Timmons, Capt. — 51, 61
Turner, Mr. — 97

V
Vance, B. H. — 5
Vance, Jas. — 123, 129

W

Walker, Maj. Gen. — 62
Walpole, Dick — 51
Walthall, Gen. — 123
Walton, Parson _____ — 4
West, Lt. — 51, 61
Wheeler, Gen. — 71, 75, 76, 81, 82, 88
Williamson, Lt. — 77, 80
Woods, Gen. — 47
Wormack, Lt. — 61

No Last Names

Dock — 51, 64, 71, 90, 102, 111
Jimmy — 51, 71, 102
Silas — 51, 71

Uncle Frank and Polly — 75, 90

Tom (a slave belonging to George Berryhill) 18, 37, 43, 44, 51, 54, 67, 69, 79, 87, 88, 91, 92, 93

Zach (a slave) — 67, 69